Labeled By Man Chosen By God

Antonio Banks

Published by Antonio Banks, 2024.

While every precaution has been taken in the preparation of this book, the publisher assumes no responsibility for errors or omissions, or for damages resulting from the use of the information contained herein.

LABELED BY MAN CHOSEN BY GOD

First edition. September 27, 2024.

Copyright © 2024 Antonio Banks.

ISBN: 979-8227933560

Written by Antonio Banks.

This book delves into how the world sees and labels us, often confining us to judgments and categories that don't reflect our true selves. Society can impose labels that define and limit us, but everything changes when we embrace a new life in Christ. In Christ, we are not bound by the labels the world assigns us. Instead, we are offered a new identity, transcending societal judgments and embracing our true, redeemed selves.

Through Christ's transformative power, our past labels and mistakes are not the final word on who we are. We are given a fresh start, a new name, and a renewed purpose. Our value and worth are defined not by the world's standards but by the love and grace of Christ. This book is a testament to the incredible transformation when we step into our new identity in Christ, where our true selves shine beyond any label the world may try to place on us. As you read these pages, may you be inspired to see beyond the labels that the world might put upon you and recognize the beautiful, renewed identity that Christ offers. Embrace the freedom and purpose that comes with this new life, and let it guide you to a future defined not by societal judgments but by the love and grace of God.

Table of Contents

Chapter 2: The Fear of The Label

Labeled By Man Chosen by God

Introduction

Losing both of my parents within two years was devastating. I still struggle daily, especially with the loss of my mother. It's not that I wasn't close to my father—I was—but I was undeniably a momma's boy. She was the one who stood by me through everything. Despite the unjust labels society placed on her, she always fought fiercely for her children.

In the sixties and seventies, interracial relationships between Caucasians and Black individuals were largely unaccepted. Couples who dared to marry or date across racial lines often faced severe repercussions and were stigmatized with cruel labels—words that I choose not to repeat here. Even her own family labeled her and kept their distance because of it. She understood all too well what it meant to bear a label many disapproved of, which led others to withdraw from her.

Now, I find myself confronting a label of my own. However, unlike hers, mine is permanent, as defined by #00591869.

Chapter 1

<u>*Now Labeled*</u>

In 2018, I found myself branded as a sex offender and a felon—a stark and harsh reality that reshaped my life in ways I could never have imagined. This new label brought stringent restrictions that profoundly altered my daily existence. The freedom to vote, obtain a carry permit, or even travel with a passport was stripped away. Simple pleasures and fundamental human interactions became restricted: I could no longer visit parks, have a girlfriend with children, or maintain friendships with anyone I didn't know before my charge. I was required to stay at least a thousand feet away from schools and playgrounds and could only attend school events with prior approval. Each year, I am burdened with a $160 fee to remain on the sex offender registry. Even the joy of decorating for Christmas or celebrating Halloween was denied to me. I was barred from serving as a pastor or attending family gatherings with friends. The list of restrictions seemed never-ending, and they remain a part of my life now and will continue to do so for the rest of my earthly existence.

The label of a violent sex offender casts a long shadow over me. Unlike other felons, the stigma attached to being labeled a sex offender is both severe and enduring. The social scorn I faced was compounded by the harshness of terms like "pedophile," "sicko," "pervert," and "Chomo" that became entwined with my identity. This intense judgment reminded me of the labels I once judged others for. Seeing my mugshot on the front page of the Lebanon Democrat was a public shaming that magnified my humiliation. The relentless dissemination of my image and personal details across social media only deepened my feelings of shame and despair. The comments and reactions I encountered were brutal and unrelenting, affirming the harsh judgment that accompanied the label I carried.

In the depths of my despair, feeling utterly hopeless, I drove to a bridge in downtown Nashville, contemplating taking my own life. As I gazed down into the void, a voice said, "It's not worth it," though I saw no one around. This profound and inexplicable moment has caused me to reflect on my life, especially my children and mother. I began to pray earnestly as I walked back to my car, seeking solace and guidance from God. Proverbs 3:5 resonated deeply: "Trust in the Lord with all your heart, and lean not on your understanding; in all your ways acknowledge Him, and He will make your paths straight." I decided to trust God completely, hoping that his divine intervention would help me navigate and overcome the heavy burden of the label I carried.

September 27th marked the beginning of my trial. By 5:00 pm that day, the judge delivered a guilty verdict and sentenced me to five years in prison, with the possibility of parole after serving 30% of the sentence. The pain and frustration of this verdict were profound. Despite my fervent prayers and belief in scriptures like John 14:13, which promises, "And whatever you ask in My name, this I will do, so that the Father may be glorified in the Son," and John 15:7, "If you remain in Me, and My words remain in you, ask whatever you wish, and it will be done for you," my request for the removal of my label was not granted. John 16:23 reassures us to "Ask the Father for whatever is in keeping with the Father I've revealed. Ask in My name, according to My will, and He'll give it to you." Despite these assurances, I struggled with the feeling that God had lost control, as John Piper aptly describes: "In our suffering, it may seem God has lost control." This feeling of abandonment and confusion was a significant part of my journey.

Yet, in this crucible of suffering, I have learned that God's plans and purposes often transcend our immediate understanding. The daily restrictions and judgment are harsh, but they have led me to a profound spiritual awakening and a deeper reliance on God's grace and strength. The transformative power of faith has provided me with a renewed sense of purpose and hope, even in the face of relentless challenges.

As you read this book, I hope you understand that while societal labels may be harsh and enduring, they do not define our ultimate worth or capacity for redemption. Embracing a new identity in Christ means recognizing that no label can diminish the profound love and grace available to us. Our value is not dictated by the world's judgments but by God's unchanging and unconditional love. Through faith and trust in Him, we can find hope and strength, transforming our lives beyond the limitations imposed by society.

Chapter 2

<u>The Fear of the Label</u>

The fear of carrying this label was overwhelming and deeply rooted in my past experiences and observations. Growing up, I witnessed my mom, grandmother, and aunt navigate relationships with men who had served time in prison. We would visit these men together, and the stories we heard about prison life were nothing short of terrifying. Our uncle, with whom we had a close bond, often shared his experiences. While some conversations were not meant for us, we overheard them. The most dreaded labels in prison—sex offender, snitch, or domestic abuser—were known to spell danger. These labels could jeopardize your life, lead to severe violence, drain your family's finances, or force you into desperate situations to secure your survival. I vividly remember my uncle recounting disturbing stories of violence, although he never explicitly mentioned rape.

When I was branded a sex offender, the fear of prison loomed large. I knew that being labeled as such would inevitably lead to incarceration. I was acutely aware that many would harbor ill will toward me, praying for misfortune or harm to befall me. The uncertainty of what might come—whether those dark wishes would come true—was paralyzing. My lack of trust in God was palpable; I felt abandoned, and I doubted whether He could protect me in a world so fraught with evil. Mentally, I braced myself for the worst, preparing for every possible scenario, though I knew my capacity to defend myself was limited.

During my year and a half in county jail, though it was relatively safer than prison, the label of sex offender set me apart from other inmates. We were isolated in a unit specifically for those with similar charges, which was intended to protect us but also kept us in a state of constant confinement. Leaving this unit was only permitted for medical appointments or visits, which required being handcuffed. We had minimal contact with the outside world, could not see from windows, and received books only once every two weeks. The isolation felt like being trapped in a cave, and the walls seemed to close in on me. My mental state began to deteriorate under the weight of this confinement.

In my desperation, I prayed fervently, asking God to grant me parole if it was His will. However, when my parole request was denied in November 2019, I felt a profound sense of betrayal. It was the second time I had trusted God, only to feel let down. Despite my disillusionment, I reached out to one of my best friends—a role model who never judged me based on my label. He was the only person who consistently answered my calls and encouraged me when I felt abandoned by God and man. His unwavering support and daily prayers were a beacon of hope during my darkest moments.

I vividly remember our conversation before my transfer to prison. I shared my plans for navigating my time behind bars, and he offered valuable advice based on his brother's experiences. He advised me to trust God despite my frustrations. When I expressed my doubts, he reminded me of scriptures that spoke to God's faithfulness: Hebrews 13:5, "God will never fail you, give you up, or leave you without support," and 1 Corinthians 10:13, "No temptation has overtaken you except what is common to humanity. And God is faithful; He will not let you be tempted beyond what you can bear." He reassured me that God had a purpose for my trials, drawing parallels with the biblical figures who faced severe challenges but were used by God in remarkable ways—Joseph, David, Moses, and Jacob.

After our conversation and his prayer, I returned to my cell with a renewed sense of purpose. Several weeks of contemplation and study led me to be baptized on March 31. This baptism felt profoundly different from previous ones, as described in Galatians 3:27, "For all of you who were baptized into Christ have clothed yourselves with

Christ." While my labels and fears did not disappear, the reassurance of God's presence became a cornerstone of my faith.

In April 2019, I requested a transfer to prison despite my mother's objections. I wanted to be home by 2023, not nearly 2025. This was a leap of faith—trusting God even without concrete evidence of the outcome. I felt guided by the Holy Spirit to make this decision and act on it.

In January 2020, I was moved to a prison in Pikeville, Tennessee. The transition was fraught with anxiety due to the dangerous environment I was entering. The prison initially felt similar to the county jail, but the reality of the situation became starkly evident when I witnessed my first stabbing. Despite the fear, I was blessed with an experienced roommate—an older inmate who provided invaluable guidance on navigating the prison environment. This wisdom was crucial, as younger inmates often posed threats or sought to involve you in risky behaviors.

Another blessing came when I secured a job after two weeks in prison. This job provided a modest income of 16 cents an hour and earned me 16 days off my sentence each month, bringing me closer to my goal of returning home. It also offered me additional freedoms—using the phone, participating in recreational activities, and more. As I grew comfortable in this environment, I began to take risks and make myself known, forgetting the dangers associated with my label.

By January, I was moved to a new prison in Hartsville, Tennessee—a place notorious for violence, rape, and overdoses. The fear of entering this "dungeon" was overwhelming, given its reputation as the worst prison in Tennessee. The atmosphere was thick with dread, and the prisoners knew your charge before you even spoke. I felt like I was being thrown into the lion's den, akin to Daniel's ordeal. Yet, just as God protected Daniel, He shielded me. Despite the prevalence of violence and abuse, I was never threatened or harmed during my three years at Hartsville. I attribute my safety to God's grace and protection, echoing Daniel 6:22, "My God sent His angel and shut the lions' mouths because I was found blameless before Him."

Through each trial and every fear, I have come to understand the depth of God's faithfulness. My journey through the darkness of labels and limitations has only highlighted the strength and resilience of trusting God.

The weight of carrying this label was immense and overwhelming, especially given my upbringing. Growing up, I watched my mom, grandmother, and aunt navigate relationships with men who had served time in prison. We would visit them together, and the tales of prison life we heard were filled with fear and foreboding. Our connection with my uncle was particularly close; he often called us when we couldn't visit. Some of the conversations we overheard were intended for adults and not for our ears, but we listened, nonetheless. The most dreaded labels in prison were sex offenders, snitches, and domestic abusers. These labels were known to bring extreme dangers—violence, rape, and the financial drain on your family. I vividly recall my uncle describing the brutal consequences of these labels, though he never explicitly mentioned the horrific details like rape. The mere thought of such a label filled me with dread.

When I was labeled a sex offender, the fear was paralyzing. I knew that this label would lead to incarceration, and I was acutely aware of the hostility and danger it would bring. The stigma associated with being a sex offender was severe; people would undoubtedly wish ill upon me and hope for my suffering. This fear of facing retribution from others was overwhelming. I found myself grappling with a deep distrust—not just toward people but toward God as well. In a world that seemed filled with evil, I struggled to believe that God could protect me. I mentally braced myself for the worst, preparing for every *conceivable scenario, though I knew my capacity to defend myself was limited.*

During my year and a half in county jail, I experienced a unique form of isolation. Although it was relatively safer than prison, being labeled a sex offender meant I was segregated from the general population. We were confined to a unit specifically for those with similar charges, which was intended to offer protection but also kept us in a state of constant confinement. Leaving this unit was restricted to medical appointments or visits requiring handcuffs. The isolation was akin to being trapped in a cave. The lack of contact with the outside world, the inability to see out of windows, and the minimal provision of books created an environment where the walls seemed to close in, and my mental health began to deteriorate.

In my desperation, I turned to prayer, asking God to grant me parole if it was His will. When my parole request was denied in November 2019, I felt a deep sense of betrayal. It was the second time I had trusted God, only to feel let down. Despite my disillusionment, I reached out to one of my best friends—a role model who had never judged me based on my label. He was the only person who consistently answered my calls and provided the encouragement I needed. His unwavering support and daily prayers were a lifeline during my darkest moments.

I vividly remember a conversation we had before my transfer to prison. I shared my plans for navigating my time behind bars, and he offered guidance based on his brother's experiences. He advised me to trust God despite my frustrations. When I expressed my doubts, he reminded me of scriptures that spoke to God's faithfulness: Hebrews 13:5, "God will never fail you, give you up, or leave you without support," and 1 Corinthians 10:13, "No temptation has overtaken you except what is common to humanity. And God is faithful; He will not let you be tempted beyond what you can bear." He reassured me that God had a purpose for my trials, drawing parallels with the biblical figures who faced severe challenges but were used by God in extraordinary ways—Joseph, David, Moses, and Jacob.

After our conversation and his prayer, I returned to my cell with a renewed sense of purpose. Several weeks of contemplation and study led me to be baptized on March 31. This baptism felt profoundly different from previous ones, as described in Galatians 3:27, "For all of you who were baptized into Christ have clothed yourselves with Christ." While my labels and fears did not disappear, the assurance of God's presence became a cornerstone of my faith.

In April 2019, I requested a transfer to prison despite my mother's objections. I wanted to be home by 2023, not nearly 2025. This was a leap of faith—trusting God even without concrete evidence of the outcome. I felt guided by the Holy Spirit to make this decision and act on it.

In January 2020, I was moved to a prison in Pikeville, Tennessee. The transition was fraught with anxiety due to the dangerous environment I was entering. The prison initially felt like the county jail, but the reality of the situation became starkly apparent when I witnessed my first stabbing. Despite the fear, I was blessed with an experienced roommate—an older inmate who provided invaluable guidance on navigating the prison environment. This wisdom was crucial, as younger inmates often posed threats or sought to involve you in risky behaviors.

Another blessing came when I secured a job after two weeks in prison. This job provided a modest income of 16 cents an hour and earned me 16 days off my sentence each month, bringing me closer to my goal of returning home. It also offered me additional freedoms—using the phone, participating in recreational activities, and more. As I grew comfortable in this environment, I began to take risks and make myself known, forgetting the dangers associated with my label.

By January, I was moved to a new prison in Hartsville, Tennessee—a place notorious for violence, rape, and overdoses. The fear of entering this "dungeon" was overwhelming, given its reputation as the worst prison in Tennessee. The atmosphere was thick with dread, and the prisoners knew your charge before you even spoke. I felt like I was being thrown into the lion's den, akin to Daniel's ordeal. Yet, just as God protected Daniel, He shielded me. Despite the prevalence of violence and abuse, I was never threatened or harmed during my three years at Hartsville. I attribute my safety to God's grace and protection, echoing Daniel 6:22, "My God sent His angel and shut the lions' mouths because I was found blameless before Him."

Through each trial and every fear, I have come to understand the depth of God's faithfulness. My journey through the darkness of labels and limitations has only highlighted the strength and resilience of trusting God. My story is one of redemption and hope, a testament to the power of faith to transform even the most harrowing of circumstances. Each step, each trial, and each victory has been a testament to God's unyielding grace and the strength that comes from believing in His promises.

Chapter 3

<u>*Everything Labeled*</u>

We live in a world where labeling has become second nature. We label people based on what we hear about them, how they look, or their past mistakes. These labels—Criminal, Deadbeat, Cheater, Liar, Idolater, Jailbird, Pedophile, Sinner, Drug Addict, Alcoholic, Homeless, Felon—are more than mere words. They can dictate who we associate with, where we can work or live, and how others perceive us. They even influence our consumer choices: an Apple loyalist might never consider an Android, while a shopper might stick to Publix or Kroger over Aldi or Cash Savers.

But why do we label everything we encounter? Labels help us quickly identify and categorize, simplifying our choices in a complex world. A label like "Frozen" in a grocery store guides us to ice cream, while "Pasta" directs us to noodles. If we want to avoid the candy aisle, we look for the "Candy" label. Labels make decision-making more accessible and shape our perceptions and interactions with people.

We extend this habit of labeling to individuals, often with damaging consequences. We place labels based on limited information or past behaviors, influencing how we treat others. For example, someone who struggled with addiction years ago might still be unfairly seen as a person with an addiction despite having turned their life around. Or someone who made a mistake early in their marriage might continue to be judged as unfaithful, even if they have since demonstrated years of loyalty and commitment.

Anais Nin's insight, "We don't see things as they are; we see them as we are," captures the essence of this issue. We impose our biases and expectations when we label someone without truly understanding them. This distorts our perception and limits our ability to see the person's true potential and value. Our brains are wired to categorize and evaluate, creating patterns that can lead to superficial judgments and missed opportunities for deeper connections.

The labels we use often fail to capture a person's true essence. They are like a book cover: important for an initial impression but not indicative of the content. Just as a beautiful book cover doesn't define the story inside, a label doesn't define a person's character or potential.

In Matthew 10:8, Jesus offers a transformative perspective: "Blessed are the pure in heart, for they shall see God." This verse reminds us that, despite societal labels and judgments, the purity of the heart truly matters. While labels can inflict pain and stigma, what should genuinely concern us is our inner character, not what others perceive.

Consider this: a person dressed in a suit and appearing successful might be struggling internally with issues like alcoholism. Conversely, someone labeled a criminal by society might have wholly transformed their life. External labels do not define our inner reality or our potential.

2 Corinthians 4:18 reinforces this understanding: "While we look not at the things which are seen, but at the things which are not seen. For the things seen are temporal, but those not seen are eternal." This passage highlights that labels and external appearances are temporary and often misleading. What truly matters is the eternal and unseen aspects of our character and our relationship with God.

The comparison between labeling people and products underscores how deeply ingrained this behavior is in our lives. We often label without realizing it, which can perpetuate stereotypes and prevent us from seeing the value in others.

The emotional and spiritual toll of these labels can be profound. Society's harsh judgments based on superficial traits or past mistakes can have significant impacts. The core message here is clear: our true worth is not defined by external labels but by the purity of our hearts and our relationship with God.

Consider the man in the suit who might be struggling internally or the criminal who has changed their mindset. These examples urge us to look beyond labels and see people for who they are. The world may impose labels based on our appearance or past actions, but God sees the true essence within us and can use us for good, regardless of society's judgments.

This message encourages empathy, understanding, and a deeper connection with others. It challenges us to break free from superficial judgments and focus on the qualities that truly matter. By looking beyond labels, we foster a more compassionate and inclusive approach to our interactions, recognizing that our value and potential are determined by our inner character and relationship with God, not by societal labels.

Imagine a world where we see beyond the surface and recognize each person's intrinsic worth regardless of their past or label. This vision invites us to embrace a more profound and transformative understanding of humanity, one where we value people for who they are at their core. It's a call to challenge our biases, foster genuine connections, and build a society that celebrates the true essence of every individual.

In this journey, let us remember that each person, regardless of their label, has the potential for redemption, growth, and greatness. By seeing and nurturing this potential, we contribute to a more compassionate and just world.

Chapter 4

You are not alone

In the rich tapestry of biblical history, many individuals were branded with societal labels that sought to define their worth and potential. Yet, these labels did not limit God's ability to use them for His divine purposes. Their stories testify to God's boundless grace and the profound truth that human judgments do not determine divine potential.

Rahab: Rahab's story is one of extraordinary faith and courage. Society labeled her as a prostitute, a label that could have quickly overshadowed her true worth and potential. However, Rahab's actions reveal a heart of extraordinary faith. When the spies from Israel entered Jericho, Rahab chose to defy her city's expectations and protect them. Her declaration in Joshua 2:9-13, "I know that the LORD has given you this land... for the LORD your God is the God in heaven above and on the earth below," was not just a statement of belief but an act of incredible courage. Despite her societal label, Rahab's faith and actions were pivotal in Jericho's conquest. Her place in the lineage of Jesus (Matthew 1:5) highlights that God's plans transcend societal labels, transforming even the most marginalized individuals into critical players in His divine narrative.

Moses: Moses' story illustrates the profound reality that God's purposes are often accomplished through flawed human vessels. Labeled a murderer after killing an Egyptian who was beating a Hebrew enslaved person, Moses fled into exile, escaping the wrath of Pharaoh. Despite this label, God had a grander vision for Moses' life. From the burning bush to the Red Sea, Moses led the Israelites from bondage to freedom, received the Ten Commandments, and guided a nation through the wilderness. His story is a testament to God's ability to redeem and repurpose even the most misunderstood and flawed individuals. It's a reminder that our past mistakes do not disqualify us from being used by God; rather, our willingness to trust and follow Him can lead to extraordinary fulfillment of His purposes.

David: King David, despite being known as a man after God's heart, faced a tumultuous journey marked by severe moral failings. His sins, including adultery with Bathsheba and orchestrating the death of her husband, Uriah, were grave and scandalous. Yet, David's story is one of profound redemption and grace. Despite his actions, God continued to use David, illustrating that His forgiveness is far-reaching. David's sincere repentance, as seen in Psalm 51, highlights the importance of acknowledging our sins and seeking forgiveness with a contrite heart. God's response to David underscores a fundamental truth: no matter our past, God's love and grace can restore and repurpose our lives for His divine plan.

Joseph: Joseph's story is a powerful narrative of betrayal, resilience, and divine timing. Falsely accused of rape and sold into slavery by his brothers, Joseph's life seemed to be one of endless suffering. Yet, his faithfulness and integrity in the face of adversity were rewarded. Joseph's interpretation of Pharaoh's dreams and subsequent rise to power in Egypt illustrate how God can use even the most unjust situations for His greater purpose. Joseph's ability to forgive his brothers and save his family from famine is a testament to the transformative power of grace. His story challenges us to see beyond labels and circumstances; trusting God is at work even in our most challenging moments.

These stories from the Bible are not isolated accounts but universal truths about human worth and divine purpose. They remind us that societal labels—whether they stem from past mistakes, moral failings, or unjust accusations—do not define our ultimate value or potential. God's grace and purpose transcend these superficial judgments, revealing a more profound truth about our identity and destiny.

Consider the story of a man who was labeled an atheist, criminal, and monster. After a violent crime, he found himself in prison, where he encountered the transformative power of God's grace. Despite facing life in prison, his sincere plea for mercy led to a reduced sentence. During his time in prison, he became a beacon of hope and faith, leading others to Christ and speaking worldwide. His life, once marked by societal judgment, became a testament to God's ability to redeem and repurpose even the most broken lives for His glory.

This chapter emphasizes that we all have a past and may struggle with feelings of inadequacy or guilt. Yet, Romans 8:28-29 offers profound reassurance: "And we know that for those who love God, all things work together for good, for those who are called according to His purpose. For those whom He foreknew, He also predestined to be conformed to the image of His Son, so that He might be the firstborn among many brothers." This passage affirms that God's sovereignty and grace ensure that every aspect of our lives is woven into His more excellent plan.

John MacArthur's observation that "No doctrine is more despised by the natural mind than the truth that GOD is sovereign" highlights the challenge of accepting this truth. Despite societal labels and judgments, God's sovereign grace sees beyond our human limitations, offering redemption and purpose that transcend our past.

In conclusion, this chapter is a powerful reminder that no label—whether assigned by society or self-imposed—can limit the transformative power of God's grace. The stories of Rahab, Moses, David, and Joseph and the modern testimony of redemption illustrate that human judgments do not confine God's purposes and plans for our lives. By focusing on what is truly important—our relationship with God and the state of our hearts—we align ourselves with His more excellent plan and embrace the boundless potential that He sees within us.

Chapter 5

<u>*Categorized by the Label*</u>

We often categorize people based on labels to simplify our world understanding. But these labels and categories can be damaging, creating division and misunderstanding, as I've experienced firsthand. Growing up biracial, I was placed in a category by my mother's Caucasian side of the family, which led to a division between us. This label also determined who I could associate with, just as my mother was labeled for being with an African American man, causing a deep rift between her and her family for many years.

This experience is not unique; it mirrors how society categorizes and labels people in harmful and limiting ways. We label others—atheist, murderer, drug addict, straight, LGBTQ+—and assume those labels define who they are. We place them into neat boxes, thinking that by doing so, we can better understand or control the world around us. But this is a mistake.

The reality is that people are more than their labels. To say, "Once a cheater, always a cheater," or "Once a thief, always a thief," ignores the complexity and potential for growth and change in every individual. Romans 3:10-12 reminds us that we are not righteous; we all have our faults and failures. Yet, we are quick to see the speck in our brother's eye while ignoring the log in our own, as Jesus warns in Matthew 7:3-5.

We've all made bad choices, but those choices don't have to define us. Some of our mistakes might not have landed us behind bars, but that doesn't mean we are without guilt. God sees all, even what others don't, and He doesn't categorize us based on our sins. Instead, Christ offers us grace and redemption, placing us all in the same category—children of God.

Galatians 3:28 reminds us, "There is neither Jew nor Greek, slave nor free, male nor female, for you are all one in Christ Jesus." On Judgment Day, we won't be separated into lines based on our labels. We will all stand before Christ, judged not by the labels society has placed on us but by our hearts and deeds.

So, no matter what labels the world gives you or what categories you've been placed in, remember that in God's eyes, you are more than a label. You are loved, valued, and capable of change. We will all be in the same line on Judgment Day, judged by Christ alone, where the only thing that will matter is what is in our hearts. Whether we hear "Depart from me, I never knew you" or "Well done, my good and faithful servant" depends not on the labels others have given us but on how we have lived our lives in faith and love.

We often categorize people based on labels to simplify and control our understanding of the world around us. But this approach is not only flawed; it's deeply damaging. My experience as someone who grew up biracial is a testament to this. My mother's Caucasian side of the family placed us into a category based solely on our mixed heritage, which created a painful division that defined many aspects of our lives. We were judged, excluded, and limited by a label that had nothing to do with who we indeed were. My mother faced harsh judgment and rejection simply because she chose to love and build a life with an African American man. This label, placed on her by her own family, created a rift that lasted for years.

This experience is not isolated. It reflects a much larger issue that plagues our society. We are quick to slap labels on others—atheist, murderer, drug addict, straight, LGBTQ+—and once those labels are in place, we assume we understand everything about that person. We categorize them, put them in a box, and think that by doing so, we can better manage our interactions with them or protect ourselves from what we don't understand. But this thinking is not just incorrect; it's destructive. It dehumanizes people, reduces their entire existence to a single word, and closes our eyes to their actual value and potential.

The reality is that people are far more complex than any label can convey. To say "Once a cheater, always a cheater" or "Once a thief, always a thief" is not only unfair—it's a denial of the truth that every person is capable of growth, change, and redemption. We all make mistakes; we all fall short. Romans 3:10-12 makes it clear: "None is righteous, no, not one; no one understands; no one seeks for God. All have turned aside; together, they have become worthless; no one does good, not even one." These words are a sobering reminder that none of us are without fault. Yet, too often, we act as if the sins and mistakes of others are somehow worse than our own. We're quick to see the flaws in others, as Jesus pointed out in Matthew 7:3-5, where He warns us against judging others while ignoring our shortcomings.

But here's the truth we often forget: Our past mistakes don't define us. We are not the total of our worst moments. Some of our errors might not have landed us behind bars, but that doesn't make us better than those with more visible mistakes. Just because the world didn't see your misstep doesn't mean it wasn't significant. God sees all and doesn't categorize us based on our sins. Instead, through Christ, He offers us grace and redemption, placing us all in the same category—His beloved children.

In Galatians 3:28, we are reminded that "There is neither Jew nor Greek, there is neither slave nor free, there is no male and female, for you are all one in Christ Jesus." This is a powerful statement that transcends all labels, all categories, and all divisions. It doesn't matter what society says about you, what box they try to put you in, or how they attempt to diminish your worth with a label. In the eyes of God, you are not a label; you are a person of immense value, created in His image, and capable of incredible things.

On Judgment Day, we won't be separated into lines based on our labels. There won't be a line for alcoholics, another for drug addicts, another for sex offenders, and so on. We will all stand before Christ, judged not by the labels society has placed on us but by our hearts and deeds. We should ask ourselves this: What kind of life are we living? Are we allowing the labels others have given us to dictate our self-worth, or are we living as people redeemed and loved by God?

When that day comes, the only judgment that will matter is God's. And He won't look at the labels; He'll look at our hearts. Whether we hear the words "Depart from me, I never knew you" or "Well done, my good and faithful servant" will depend not on the categories the world placed us in but on how we chose to live our lives, how we treated others, and how we followed God's call.

*So, let's reject the labels. Let's stop categorizing people as if a single word can fully know them. Let's remember that every person we meet is more than their past, their mistakes, and more than what society says they are. Let's live in the truth that we are all one in Christ Jesus and *treat each other with the love, respect, and dignity that truth demands. You are more than a label; you are a child of God, the only identity that truly matters.*

Chapter 6

Beyond the Label

2 Corinthians 5:17 says, "Therefore if anyone is in Christ, he is a new creation. The old has passed away; behold, the new has come. All this is from God, who reconciled us to himself and gave us the ministry of reconciliation through Christ." This powerful verse is a declaration of hope and transformation—a reminder that in Christ, we are not bound by our past, our mistakes, or the labels the world has placed upon us. It's an invitation to embrace a new identity, one that is rooted in God's grace and love.

But how do we live out this new identity when the world constantly tries to remind us of our old selves? How do we hold onto the truth that we are a new creation in Christ when our past mistakes are thrown back in our faces, when society insists on defining us by the worst things we've ever done or by labels that do not reflect who we are in God's eyes?

This struggle is something I grapple with daily. It often feels like living with a spiritual form of leprosy, much like those in biblical times who were shunned, feared, and labeled as unclean. Lepers were seen as the embodiment of sin, cut off from society and forced to live in isolation. They had to announce their uncleanliness whenever they approached others, a constant reminder of their rejection and their separation from God and people.

In many ways, this is how society treats us today when we carry specific labels. Society can be ruthless in its judgment, quick to label, and slow to forgive. These labels can feel like a curse, a scarlet letter we carry wherever we go. They can make us feel worthless, rejected, and isolated, just like the lepers of old. It's as if we are constantly forced to announce our unworthiness before we even have a chance to show who we are.

I remember my mother's battle with a severe skin condition called psoriasis. Though not contagious, it was visibly alarming to others. I recall the way people would stare at her, the way some doctors hesitated to touch her, and how others would avoid her altogether, labeling her as unclean because of what they saw on the surface. She would cover her arms with long sleeves, hiding her condition, not because she was ashamed of who she was but because she wanted to avoid the judgmental stares and whispered remarks.

Similarly, when society labels us, it can make us want to hide parts of ourselves, retreat into isolation, and cover up our true identity in Christ. But we cannot allow these labels to define us. We cannot let the world's perception dictate our self-worth. We are called to live boldly in the truth of who we are in Christ—a new creation free from the chains of our past.

It's easy for someone to say, "Who cares what people think?" But the reality is that most of us do care. We long to be accepted, belong, and find our place. It's a natural human desire to connect with others and be seen and loved for who we are. But the question is, how do we manage not to let the opinions of others and the labels they impose on us affect how we see ourselves?

Proverbs 23:7 says, "For as he thinketh in his heart, so is he." This verse reminds us that our identity is shaped by what we believe about ourselves in our hearts. The world is a whole of hypocrites—people who may appear righteous on the outside but are filled with darkness and brokenness on the inside. Jesus warned us about these people, particularly in religious circles, where appearances often matter more than the condition of the heart.

Churches, too, can be places where labels and judgments are handed out freely. They are often full of people who are quick to point out the speck in someone else's eye while ignoring the log in their own. But if we recognize that even those who judge us are broken and in need of grace, we can move beyond the fear of their opinions. We can start to see them not as the ultimate authority on our worth but as fellow humans who are just as in need of God's mercy as we are.

It's like going to marriage counseling and pretending that everything is perfect when, in reality, there are deep issues that need to be addressed. If we were truly perfect, we wouldn't need counseling. In the same way, if the world were entirely of perfect people, we wouldn't need grace. But the truth is, we all need God's grace, and we must learn to extend that same grace to ourselves and others, regardless of the labels placed upon us.

The world will always try to label us, but we cannot let that define who we are. Jesus Himself warned us about the dangers of false prophets and hypocrites, those who may appear righteous but are inwardly corrupt. Matthew 7:15-23, He says, "Beware of false prophets, who come to you in sheep's clothing but inwardly are ravenous wolves. You will recognize them by their fruits. Are grapes gathered from thornbushes or figs from thistles? So, every healthy tree bears good fruit, but the diseased tree bears bad fruit. A healthy tree cannot bear bad fruit, nor can a diseased tree bear good fruit. Every tree that does not bear good fruit is cut down and thrown into the fire. Thus, you will recognize them by their fruits. Not everyone who says to me, 'Lord, Lord,' will enter the kingdom of heaven, but the one who does the will of my Father who is in heaven."

These verses remind us that while people may judge us based on our labels, God looks at the fruit of our lives—the actual evidence of who we are in Him. Some people will never be able to see past the label, but that's okay because their opinions do not determine our worth. What matters is how we live our lives by God's will.

On Judgment Day, we will all stand before Christ, and He will not separate us based on the labels the world has given us. He won't categorize us into lines based on our past mistakes or the names others have called us. Instead, He will look at our hearts, actions, and whether we followed Him faithfully. Those who have trusted in Christ *and lived as new creations will hear, "Well done, my good and faithful servant."*

So, let us live in the freedom that Christ has given us, knowing that we are not defined by our past or by the labels others place on us. We are defined by God's love, His grace, and the new life we have in Him. Let us stand firm in this truth, confident in our identity as children of God, and live boldly as new creations, free from the chains of our old selves.

Chapter 7

Living with the Label

Living with the label of a sex offender is an experience that few can truly understand, and it's a burden that I have to carry every day. This isn't something I'm proud of—far from it. This label is a heavy, relentless shadow that follows me wherever I go, dictating my life in ways that many would find unimaginable. It's not just a label; it's a life sentence that impacts every relationship, every interaction, and every thought.

The rules and regulations that come with this label are extensive and unforgiving. They reach every corner of my life, restricting where I can go, who I can be with, and what I can do. I can't go to places that others can. I can't date anyone with children if I didn't know them before my conviction. I can't even befriend someone with children unless we are already friends. These rules aren't temporary—they are with me for the rest of my life, a constant reminder of my past and a barrier to any semblance of everyday life.

One of the most complex parts of living with this label is its impact on my relationship with my children. My youngest son and I have managed to maintain a good father-son relationship, but my older sons and daughters are estranged from me. The label complicates everything. It's not just that I wasn't a great father; the label has made it nearly impossible to repair those relationships. The label is like a wall between us, which sometimes feels insurmountable.

But the label doesn't just affect my relationships—it affects my mind. It creates a sense of paranoia, a constant feeling that everyone knows who I am and what I've done. I walk through life with the assumption that my label is written on my forehead for all to see. Even when I logically know that most people don't know my past, the label still whispers in my ear, making me doubt and fear.

I remember the first time I went to a church group after leaving prison. I was anxious, unsure of how I would be received. I waited outside until I saw someone else arrive, a woman who asked me, "Who invited you?" Immediately, my mind went into overdrive. I assumed she knew my background and was questioning why someone like me would be there. I almost left right then and there. But I didn't. I walked into the house, saw the host and his wife, and recognized the man who had invited me. Yet, I couldn't shake the feeling of unease. My anxiety shot through the roof, and I found myself standing with my back against the wall, watching everyone, waiting for some sign that they knew who I was. In reality, maybe only two people in that room knew about my label, but in my mind, it felt like everyone knew.

This is the reality of living with a label like this. It affects how others see you and how you see yourself. It's a constant battle between wanting to connect with others and fearing being judged or rejected. The label is always there, like a chain around your neck, reminding you of your past and making it difficult to move forward.

But here's the thing: I know I'm not alone in this struggle. Countless others live with labels—whether it's sex offender, addict, criminal, or any other label society places on us. We all face the same battle. We all know what it's like to be defined by our worst moments, to have our entire lives reduced to a single word or phrase. But we also know that those labels don't have to define us.

Romans 12:2 says, "Do not be conformed to this world, but be transformed by the renewal of your mind." This verse is a lifeline, a reminder that we are more than the labels society gives us. In Christ, we are new creations. The old has passed away, and the new has come. This is a truth that I cling to every day. It's a reminder that my past does not define my future. Yes, the label is still there and affects my *life profoundly. But it doesn't have to control me. It doesn't have to dictate who I am or what I become.*

The world will always be quick to judge and quick to label. But we must remember that our time here on Earth is temporary. The struggles and afflictions we face now are momentary compared to the eternal glory that awaits us. As 2 Corinthians 4:17-18 says, "For this light momentary affliction is preparing for us an eternal weight of glory beyond all comparison." This perspective is what gives me hope. It reminds me that while the label may feel overwhelming now, it's not the end of the story. A greater purpose and glory awaits us if we remain faithful.

John Piper's words resonate deeply: "People don't enjoy salt. They want what is salted. We are the salt of the earth. We do not exist for ourselves." This is a powerful reminder that our lives, even with the labels we carry, have a purpose. We are here to make a difference, to be the salt that adds flavor to the lives of others. And in doing so, we can find meaning and hope, even amid our struggles.

Living with this label is problematic. It's a daily battle against fear, shame, and the judgment of others. But I am determined not to let it define me. I am determined to live a pleasing life to God, to be the salt of the earth, and to make a difference in the lives of others. Yes, the label is there, but so is God's grace. And that is more powerful than any label the world can place on me.

I have realized that God's purpose for my life is greater than the label I carry. He has called me to be more than what society says I am. He has called me to be a light in the darkness, a testimony of His grace and redemption. And that is what I strive to be every day. No matter how heavy the label feels or how often I stumble or fall, I know God is with me. He is my strength, my refuge, and my hope. And with Him, I can overcome anything.

So, I want to tell anyone living with a label: You are not alone. Your label does not define you. God has a purpose for your life that is greater than anything the world can say about you. Trust, lean on Him, and let Him transform your mind and heart. The journey won't be easy, but it will be worth it. In the end, you will see that God's grace is sufficient, His love is unending, and His purpose for your life is more significant than anything you can imagine.

Chapter 8

<u>*Associating with Someone Labeled*</u>

Believe it or not, when someone carries a negative label, it doesn't just affect them; it extends its reach, touching the lives of everyone associated with them. This is a reality I know all too well. The impact of a label is not confined to the individual—its shadow looms over their family, friends, and acquaintances. The world, so quick to judge, often fails to see the truth beyond the surface. It assumes, categorizes, and stigmatizes the person and everyone connected to them. It's like a ripple effect, spreading and contaminating everything.

Consider the situation where you know someone who has struggled with drugs. Even if they've turned their life around, just being close to them can cause people to look at you differently. Society might question your integrity, lifestyle, and choices even though you've done nothing wrong. That's the power of a label—it doesn't just mark the person who wears it; it has the potential to brand everyone in their orbit. This can strain relationships, breed distrust, and create an invisible barrier between you and the rest of the world. The harsh reality is that even the most innocent associations can bring unwarranted suspicion and prejudice.

Imagine being friends with someone who has a history of alcohol abuse. If they invite you out for a night at a bar, and you go along to keep them company, people might start whispering about your drinking habits. It doesn't matter that you only sipped on a Coke or a sweet tea all night—guilt by association is all too real in this world. The same applies to any label—cheater, liar, or criminal. If someone close to you carries that label, the world will quickly judge you by the same standard. You might find yourself losing friends, being judged by family, or seeing your children treated differently, all because of someone else's past. It's an unfair burden to bear, but it's a reality we must face.

But let's be clear: this phenomenon isn't new. It's as old as time itself. Even Jesus Christ, the sinless Son of God, was judged and labeled because of the people He chose to associate with. Despite His perfection, He was scorned for befriending sinners, tax collectors, and outcasts. But Jesus never let the world's labels dictate His actions or diminish His love. He looked beyond the surface, beyond the labels, and saw the hearts of the people. Where others saw disgrace, He saw potential. Where others saw sin, He saw the opportunity for redemption.

Take, for example, the Samaritan woman at the well. In her society, she was labeled a fornicator because she lived with a man who wasn't her husband. Worse still, she was a Samaritan, a group despised by the Jews. Samaritans were seen as the lowest of the low, unworthy of any respect or association. But Jesus didn't care about the societal rules or the labels others had placed on her. He didn't see a fornicator or a despised Samaritan; He saw a woman needing love, forgiveness, and redemption. Jesus spoke to her, acknowledged her worth, and offered her eternal life. In doing so, He shattered society's labels on her, showing that His love transcends all human judgment.

Consider also the leper that Jesus healed. According to the laws of that time, no one was supposed to come near a leper, let alone touch them. Lepers were considered unclean and untouchable and were forced to live in isolation. But when Jesus encountered a leper who begged for healing, He didn't hesitate. Jesus could have healed him with just a word from a distance, but He chose to reach and touch him. In that moment, Jesus demonstrated His boundless compassion and willingness to break societal norms to show love and healing. He didn't see the " unclean " label—He saw a person who needed His touch, love, and healing power.

This is the truth we must hold onto. Yes, the world is quick to label, judge, and shun. But we serve a God who sees beyond the labels. He sees the heart, and He loves us with an everlasting love that is not dependent on our past or the labels society places on us. No matter what label we carry or how heavy it feels, we must remember that God's love is more significant. His grace is sufficient, and His power to redeem and restore is beyond anything the world can comprehend.

Living with a label in this world is undoubtedly challenging. It can feel like a heavy burden, a constant reminder of past mistakes or unjust judgments. But we are not defined by the world's labels. God's love and grace define us. Through Christ's sacrifice on the cross, our sins have been wiped clean and made new. As 1 John 1:9 says, "God is faithful and just to forgive us our sins and to cleanse us from all unrighteousness." This promise is not conditional on how the world sees us; it's based on our faith in Christ and His finished work on the cross.

Isaiah 51:12 offers us further assurance: "I, I am he who comforts you; who are you that you are afraid of man who dies, of the son of man who is made like grass?" In this verse, God reminds us that He is our comforter, protector, provider, and peace. We have nothing to fear from the judgments or labels of this world. The opinions of others are fleeting, like grass that withers and fades, but God's love and promises endure forever.

To anyone struggling with a label—whether it's one you carry yourself or one that affects you through association—I want to encourage you today. You are not defined by what the world says about you. Your identity is not tied to a label, a past mistake, or the judgments of others. You are defined by what God says about you. And He says that you are loved, you are forgiven, you are redeemed, and you are His. The labels of this world may feel heavy, but they are not the ultimate truth. The ultimate truth is found in God's Word, promises, and love for you.

Remember, the world may see the label, but God sees your heart. He sees your potential, your worth, and your value. He sees you as His beloved child; nothing can take that away from you. So, hold your head high, trust in God's promises, and live in the confidence that you are loved and accepted by the Creator of the universe. The labels the world tries to place on you may be burdensome, but they are nothing compared to the freedom and joy found in Christ. Trust in Him, lean on Him, and let His love and grace be the truth that defines your life. You are more than a label—you are a new creation in Christ, which is the truth that matters most.

Chapter 9

Growing with The Label

How can we grow with a label when society wants us to wither away? This is a question that many of us face daily, especially when the world seems determined to define us by our past mistakes, our shortcomings, and the labels they've placed upon us. It's as though we're trying to nurture a seedling in a harsh desert, where every attempt at growth is met with scorn and doubt. Society's whispers are often louder than our inner voice, saying, "I told you so," or "You can't change." It's a battle, not a battle we face alone.

This struggle to grow is not unique to our time. Throughout history, those who have sought transformation, redemption, and a new path have been met with resistance. Jesus Himself warned us of this when He said, "If the world hates you, keep in mind that it hated me first" (John 15:18). The world is not kind to those who dare to defy the labels it imposes. Whether it's overcoming an addiction, changing a lifestyle, or simply trying to live a life of faith in a world that scoffs at it, the road is never easy. But we are not called to an easy road; we are called to a road that leads to life.

Consider the Apostle Paul, formerly known as Saul. His story is one of the most powerful testimonies of the transformative power of Christ. Saul was a Pharisee, a man deeply rooted in the traditions of Judaism, and he was zealous in his persecution of Christians. His mission was to destroy the early Church, and he did so with ruthless efficiency. To those early Christians, Saul was a terror, a man whose name struck fear into their hearts. Many believed he would never change—his path was set, and his fate sealed.

But God had other plans. On the road to Damascus, Saul encountered the risen Christ in a blinding vision that changed everything. In that moment, Saul became Paul, a new creation in Christ. His transformation was so radical that it shocked everyone who knew him. The man who had once persecuted Christians became one of the most passionate advocates for the Gospel. Paul's letters, which form a significant portion of the New Testament, continue to inspire and guide Christians to this day, a testament to the enduring power of faith and the transformative nature of God's grace. His story is a beacon of hope, showing that no one is beyond the reach of God's grace.

Yet, even after his conversion, Paul was not accessible from the label of his past. Many still remembered him as the man who had persecuted the Church. He was mistrusted and feared, and his past was a constant shadow. But Paul did not let his label define him. He knew that he was a new creation in Christ, and he lived out his faith boldly, proclaiming the message he once sought to destroy. This stark contrast between his past and present, Saul who persecuted and Paul who preached, is a powerful testament to the transformative power of faith.

The story of Paul teaches us that no label is too strong for God to break, and no past is too dark for God to redeem. When we surrender to Christ, we become new creations, just as Paul did. The old has passed away, and the new has come. This is the promise of 2 Corinthians 5:17, and it's for all of us, regardless of what the world may say.

But Paul is not the only example. Rahab, the prostitute from Jericho, is another powerful testament to the grace and mercy of God. Rahab was a woman with a past, a label, and a reputation. She was part of a corrupt society, living a life many would have judged harshly. But when the opportunity came, Rahab chose to help the Israelite spies, risking her life. Her faith and courage led to her being spared when Jericho fell. More than that, Rahab was grafted into the lineage of Christ, becoming the great-great-grandmother of King David and, ultimately, part of the genealogy of Jesus Himself.

Rahab's story shows us that God doesn't see us like the world does. He looks beyond our labels, mistakes, and pasts and sees our potential, faith, and hearts. Where society sees a prostitute, God sees a woman of faith. When society sees a murderer, God considers them an apostle. This is the radical, transformative power of God's grace.

But how do we live in this truth when society constantly reminds us of our labels? How do we grow when the world seems to keep us in the box it has placed us in? The answer lies in our relationship with Christ. We must root ourselves in His Word, immerse ourselves in His promises, and surround ourselves with His people. It's not enough to know that we are new creations; we must live it out every day, even when it's hard, even when the world doesn't recognize it.

Ephesians 2:8 says, "For by grace you have been saved through faith. And this is not your own doing; it is the gift of God." Our salvation, our new identity in Christ, is not something we earn or achieve. It is a gift freely given by a loving God. This truth should fill us with confidence and courage. It is not our past that defines us, but the grace of God that saves us.

And this grace is not just for us; it's for those around us. When we live out our new identity in Christ, we become a testimony to others. Our lives become a reflection of God's redeeming power. We may still carry the labels that society has placed on us, but those labels no longer have the power to define us. We are defined by Christ, His love, His sacrifice, and His resurrection.

Isaiah 51:12 reminds us, "I, I am he who comforts you; who are you that you are afraid of man who dies, of the son of man who is made like grass?" We serve a God who is far greater than any label, any past, or any fear. He is our comfort, our strength, and our shield.

We find the courage to grow and flourish in Him, even in the face of opposition.

And let us not forget, as John Piper wisely said, "People don't enjoy salt. They want what is salted. We are the salt of the earth. We do not exist for ourselves." Our lives are meant to reflect Christ to the world. We are called to be salt and light, to bring the flavor of God's grace and truth to a world that desperately needs it. We have a unique testimony to share even with our labels or perhaps because of them. Our transformation journey of growing in Christ despite the labels can inspire others to seek the same grace and redemption we have found.

We will always face challenges, opposition, and doubt in this world. But we must remember that our time here is temporary. As 2 Corinthians 4:17-18 says, "For this light momentary affliction is preparing for us an eternal weight of glory beyond all comparison, as we look not to the things that are seen but to the unseen things. The things seen are transient, but the unseen things are eternal." Our focus must remain on the eternal, the promises of God, and the hope we have in Christ.

So, how do we grow with a label when society wants us to wither away? We grow by rooting ourselves in Christ, trusting His promises, and living out our new identity daily. We grow by refusing to let the world's labels define us and by embracing the truth of who we are in Christ. We grow by becoming salt and light, by allowing our lives to be a testimony to the transformative power of God's grace. And we grow by keeping our eyes on the eternal, knowing that our present struggles are nothing compared to the glory that awaits us in Christ.

Chapter 10

Worthy or Unworthy, Though Labeled

Do you ever feel unworthy because of the labels society has placed on you? It's a profound and painful experience that can make you question your value and place. But what does it indeed mean to be unworthy? At its core, being deemed unworthy implies being considered unfit, undeserving, or not good enough. Society often imposes these labels, categorizing people based on their past actions or present struggles, making it seem like some individuals are forever defined by their mistakes.

For example, society might view those convicted of severe crimes, such as murder, as irredeemable. They may think that people with addiction issues or those facing homelessness are unworthy of respect and compassion. These judgments are often harsh and unforgiving, deeply embedded in societal attitudes. Conversations about notorious criminals usually reveal a common sentiment: many believe those who have committed serious crimes are beyond redemption or rehabilitation. Even when individuals who have committed grave offenses experience a genuine transformation and embrace faith, they are frequently met with skepticism. Their past actions and societal labels seem to overshadow their efforts to change, creating a barrier to forgiveness and acceptance.

However, God's perspective on worthiness is radically different from society's. While human judgments are often rigid and unforgiving, God's view is filled with grace and mercy. God does indeed define sin—if you have stolen, you are labeled a thief; if you have committed rape, you are labeled a rapist; if you have taken a life, you are labeled a murderer. God does not overlook sin; it is acknowledged, and the penalty is severe. In the eyes of a holy God, sin must be paid for, and the cost is death. This truth applies universally, regardless of the nature or extent of the sin.

Yet, here's the incredible truth: when we bring our sins and labels to Jesus Christ, everything changes. Jesus Christ took upon Himself the punishment meant for us. He bore the weight of our sins and the labels we carry. Romans 10:13 proclaims, "Everyone who calls on the name of the Lord will be saved." This promise is not limited to those with a clean record or a spotless past. It extends to everyone—every ethnicity, background, and history. But this promise requires genuine faith and repentance.

The astonishing reality of Christ's sacrifice is that He not only bears our sins but also the labels associated with them. When Jesus died on the cross, He didn't just die for some sins—He died for every sin, every label, and every mistake we've ever made. Through His sacrifice, the burden of our past is lifted. When God looks at us after we place our trust in Jesus, He no longer sees the labels of our past. He sees His beloved children, cleansed and justified by the grace of Christ.

This grace is not just a momentary relief but a profound transformation. In Christ, we are made new. Our worth is determined not by societal judgments or past mistakes but by God's incredible love and grace. No matter how unworthy you may feel or how heavy the labels of your past may be, Jesus offers you a chance to be made new.

Imagine the freedom of living beyond societal labels, embracing a new identity rooted in Christ's love. This grace doesn't just redefine us; it empowers us to live with purpose, hope, and confidence. We are not defined by our past but by our relationship with God. Our worth is anchored in His boundless love and redeeming grace.

So, if you find yourself burdened by labels and doubts about your worthiness, remember this: God's view of you far exceeds any human judgment. He sees your heart, knows your potential, and offers redemption to all who seek it. Embrace this truth with confidence. Let the grace of Christ transform you and renew your sense of worth. Live boldly in the knowledge that, in Christ, you are cherished, redeemed, and worthy of a future filled with hope and purpose.

In the grand scheme of eternity, the labels that once seemed so defining will fade away. What remains is the unshakable truth of who you are in Christ: a beloved child of God, made whole and set free. Embrace this identity with pride and live each day knowing that your worth is not measured by the world's standards but by the immeasurable love of God.

Chapter 11

<u>Head-to-Head with The Label</u>

I remember growing up with my older brother and our countless sports battles. We were always on different teams, separated by years and skill levels. But the stars aligned when we ended up on the same high school football team. It was like a dream come true—we could finally practice together, share victories, and engage in sibling trash talk that would make even the most seasoned athletes cringe.

One memorable day at practice, our coach caught us in the middle of one of our infamous banter sessions. Seeing an opportunity for some high-energy competition, he suggested a one-on-one showdown to settle our trash talk once and for all. We eagerly agreed, thinking we were about to make football history. We lined up—me as the wide receiver, him as the lineman. The coach blew the whistle, and we charged at each other. I was on my back in seconds, feeling like a ragdoll in a wind tunnel. My brother, a solid 220 pounds of muscle and determination, had me easily pinned down. I was 125 pounds of sheer bravado, and my bravado didn't stand a chance.

This epic clash vividly portrays the overwhelming nature of carrying a societal label. It's like being pitted against Goliath, except instead of a giant warrior, you're grappling with judgment, stereotypes, and misconceptions that feel as heavy as a ton of bricks. Imagine David standing against Goliath; only this time, it's a colossal stack of societal expectations and doubts. It's no wonder David must have felt like he was going up against a wall made of reinforced steel; the weight of societal labels can be crushing.

The Israelites were petrified when they saw Goliath; honestly, I think they had a good reason. Goliath wasn't just tall; he was the walking embodiment of every nightmare you'd ever had about being overpowered. And when society labels you, it can feel like you're facing your own Goliath—an insurmountable obstacle that mocks your every attempt to break free.

But let's think about David for a second. This young shepherd boy was chosen to face the giant, and he wasn't equipped with a fancy suit of armor or a high-tech sling. He had a slingshot and a rock, which sounded like something a kid would use to fend off an overzealous squirrel, not a giant. Yet, David faced Goliath with unwavering faith, and that's the key takeaway. He didn't just show up with a slingshot; he showed up with God on his side.

Society often doubts us, much like the Israelites doubted David. They see the labels, judgments, and past mistakes and think, "Oh, this will be easy to dismiss." They might look at us like Goliath looked at David—dismissive, mocking, and confident that we're not worth their attention. But here's the thing: there's a much bigger giant in our corner than any label society can throw at us. That giant is God.

As David had faith in facing Goliath, we have God's promises to face our societal labels. He tells us in 2 Chronicles 20:17, "Do not be afraid or discouraged because of this vast army. For the battle is not yours, but God's." Imagine God is like your heavyweight champion, fighting battles you didn't even know you had entered. Exodus 14:14 assures us, "The Lord will fight for you; you need only to be still." It's like having a superpower that kicks in when you need it most instead of flying or turning invisible; it's God's unwavering support and love.

When society throws labels at us, it's like getting hit with a giant snowball of negativity. And while it might sting for a moment, it's important to remember that snowballs eventually melt. Our labels might seem permanent, but they're not. They're like the frosty remnants of an old storm, soon to be washed away by the sun of God's grace and mercy.

Let's face it: battling societal labels can feel like wrestling with a bear while juggling flaming torches. It's challenging and overwhelming; sometimes, the universe conspires against you. But that's where faith comes in. Just as David didn't back down from Goliath, we shouldn't back down from society's challenges. Instead, we stand firm, trusting that God is working behind the scenes, turning what seems like an impossible fight into a testimony of His power.

So, the next time you feel overwhelmed by your label, remember you're not alone in the ring. You've got a divine coach in your corner, and He's got plans to help you overcome every obstacle. Embrace your inner David, sling your faith with confidence, and trust that God's got the giant of societal judgment in a headlock. With God on your side, every battle is winnable, every label is conquerable, and every giant is just another opportunity to witness the incredible power of God's grace.

Chapter 12

The Battle is Not Yours

This chapter might be a bit of a journey, so grab a coffee or, if you're like me, a cherry Coke and settle in. We're diving into a topic that's as universal as it is personal: battles. And by "battles," I don't just mean the kind with swords and shields—although those are undoubtedly dramatic! Battles refer to military conflicts, relationship struggles, life challenges, sports competitions, political disputes, church conflicts, etc. Let's face it: battles are everywhere, and the unfortunate reality is that while we might win some, we also lose some. Some people seem to breeze through life, winning every fight, while others feel like they're constantly on the losing end. And then there are the battles we don't even choose to fight; they're thrust upon us, or worse, upon those we love.

Have you ever found yourself wanting to fight someone else's battle? I'm willing to bet that 99% of moms, dads, daughters, and sons would say they'd switch places with a loved one in a heartbeat if it meant they could fight their battles for them. I know I would. Something in us compels us to step in, to take the hits if it means sparing those we care about. We're wired that way, aren't we? We can't help but want to protect and fight for the ones we love.

I vividly remember the pain in my dad's voice when he was battling cancer. He was undergoing dialysis, a grueling process that left him weak and tired. I could only say, "Dad, you know if I could take your spot, I would." His response was always the same: "Boy, you are crazy." And my reply was always, "Yes, I am." But that wasn't just empty talk; I meant every word. I would have done it in a second if

I could have taken his place. Many of you reading this would do the same for your loved ones, no questions asked.

My mom faced her painful battle with psoriasis. Watching her suffer was one of the hardest things I've ever experienced. Her skin would flare up, turning red and sore, and there was nothing I could do but sit with her and share in her suffering. We'd cry together, both of us wishing there was something—anything—that could ease her pain. All I could offer was the same thing I'd offered my dad: "I wish I could take your place."

And then there's a man I know at work whose daughter has been battling a flesh-eating parasite on her scalp for five years. Can you even imagine? Open sores, hair loss, constant pain—and no cure or even a known cause. He's watched his daughter suffer day in and day out, and every day, he tells me the same thing: "I would do anything to take her place." That kind of love makes you willing to do the impossible and leaves you feeling helpless because, despite your willingness, you can do nothing to change the situation.

But the truth is, as much as we want to fight these battles for our loved ones, sometimes we're reminded that we're not in control. That's a tough pill to swallow, especially for those who like to fix things, to be the one who steps in and makes it all better. But the reality is that some battles are beyond our reach—they belong to God.

The Bible consists of stories about battles; not all have clear-cut victories. Take Exodus 1:15-17, for example. The Egyptians were so afraid of the Israelites' growing numbers that they ordered the Hebrew midwives to kill all the male children born to Israelite women, leaving only the daughters. That's a battle with stakes higher than most of us can imagine. Or consider the classic struggle between David and Goliath. Just like a young shepherd, David faced a giant warrior who was the epitome of invincibility. Then there's the story of Joseph and his brothers, who, driven by jealousy, sold him into slavery—a battle of betrayal that seemed to have no winners. But in all these stories, something greater was at work beyond the immediate struggle.

You see, these battles weren't just physical; they were spiritual. And the ultimate victory didn't belong to the warriors or the strategists but to God. In 1 Samuel 17:45, David tells Goliath, "You come against me with sword and spear and javelin, but I come against you in the name of the Lord Almighty, the God of the armies of Israel, whom you have defied." David knew the battle wasn't his; it was God's. The Hebrew midwives in Exodus 1:17 defied the king of Egypt, risking their lives to save the male children because they feared God more than they feared the king. Even Joseph's story, which seemed like a series of tragic events, was ultimately a victory for God. Genesis 39:2 tells us, "The Lord was with Joseph," and because of that, everything that happened to him was part of God's more excellent plan.

Life is full of battles we didn't ask for, and sometimes, it feels like we're fighting Goliath every day. Let's be honest: who among us hasn't felt like David at some point—small, outnumbered, and outmatched? Whether it's financial struggles, family health problems, addiction issues, or the loss of loved ones, these battles are real, and they're tough. When we fight them on our own, we often lose. But here's the promise we can hold onto: Exodus 14:14 says, "The Lord will fight for you; you need only to be still." And in 2 Chronicles 20:15, we're reminded, "The battle is not yours, but God's." This doesn't mean life will be easy or we won't face trials. 2 Timothy 3:12 clarifies: "Indeed, all who desire to live godly in Christ Jesus will be persecuted." But it also means that the ultimate victory isn't up to us; it's in God's hands.

And isn't that a relief? Because let's face it, we're not equipped to win every battle. We don't have the strength, the wisdom, or the resources to fight every giant that comes our way. But the good news is, we don't have to. God has promised to fight for us. He's the one who *steps in when we're weakest and takes up our cause when we're out of options. And if there's one thing we know about God, He never loses.*

Think about it: the God who parted the Red Sea, brought down the walls of Jericho, and turned a shepherd boy into a king—He's the same God who fights for you. So, when you're feeling overwhelmed, when the battle seems too big, and the odds are stacked against you, remember that you're not in this alone. God is with you, and He's fighting on your behalf.

It's easy to feel like the world is against you, especially when society labels you as something you're not. Maybe you've been labeled as unworthy, hopeless, or defeated. Perhaps you've been told that you're not good enough, that you'll never measure up. But here's the thing: God doesn't see you like the world does. He sees you as His child, His beloved, and His warrior. And those labels don't stand a chance when God is on your side.

I remember that time in high school when I finally got to go head-to-head with my older brother on the football field. I was sure I could take him even though he was twice my size. I was full of confidence, even a little cocky, until I found myself flat on my back, staring up at the sky, wondering what just happened. My brother had wiped the field with me, and all my trash talk suddenly seemed less impressive. But you know what? Even though I lost that battle, I got back up. I kept playing, kept practicing, and eventually, I got stronger. That's what life is like sometimes. We go head-to-head with giants and sometimes end up flat on our backs. But the important thing is to get back up, knowing we're not going in alone the next time.

So, whether you fight for yourself or someone you love, remember that your strength will not win the day. It's God's. Trust, lean on Him, and let Him fight for you. And when you do, you'll find that the giants aren't as big as they seem, and the battles aren't as impossible as they feel.

Remember Psalm 20:7: "Some trust in chariots and some in horses, but we trust in the name of the Lord our God." No matter what society labels you or how many battles you've lost in the past, God is fighting for you, and He's never lost a battle yet. So, take a deep breath, hold your head high, and keep going. God got this one. And who knows? Maybe one day, you'll look back on this battle and see how God used it to make you stronger, wiser, and more like Him. After all, if He can turn a shepherd boy into a king, there's no limit to what He can do in your life.

Chapter 13

It's Not Rejection It's Redirection

Rejection is one of those inevitable experiences that no one can escape, no matter who you are or where you come from. It's a universal experience that can leave a lasting impact and doesn't discriminate. Whether it's rejection from a romantic partner, a job, a sports team, a college, a community, or even from a church—the sting of being told "no" can cut deep. I've seen people who were sure they'd be paroled and finally return home to their families, only to face the crushing disappointment of rejection. It makes you feel utterly useless, helpless, and hopeless. I know that feeling all too well, having experienced rejection myself, mainly due to the label I carry.

Rejection has existed since the dawn of time, and the Bible is an entire story of people who faced it, just like we do today. Take Hannah, for example. She was ridiculed and tormented by her husband's other wife because she couldn't have children. The Bible tells us that the Lord had closed her womb, and this caused Hannah so much distress that she was driven to tears, unable to eat or sleep (1 Samuel 1:7). Then there's Paul—formerly known as Saul—who was rejected and persecuted after his dramatic conversion to Christianity. He went from being the persecutor to the persecuted, facing rejection from those who once welcomed him with open arms (Acts 14:19). Jeremiah, the weeping prophet, was rejected, persecuted, and imprisoned by the very people he was trying to help—delivering God's messages to Judah, only to be met with anger and violence (Jeremiah 20:2). Moses, too, faced rejection when he first tried to intervene on behalf of the Hebrews and later from Pharaoh himself (Exodus 2:14). And let's not forget Jesus, our Lord, and Savior, who was rejected by

His people and endured immense suffering, ultimately being crucified (John 1:11).

These biblical figures faced rejection from all sides, just as we sometimes do. It can come from those closest to us—our children, parents, spouses, or even friends. For me, the most painful rejections have come from two of my four kids, whom I haven't seen in years, all because of the label I carry. It's a heartache that doesn't go away. But here's the thing: as painful as rejection is, it doesn't define us. One person's rejection doesn't mean we are unlovable, unworthy, or without value. It's easy to forget this when we're in the thick of it. Still, as believers, we must remember that we have a God who loves us unconditionally, without reservation or hesitation.

When born again, we are accepted—entirely, wholly, and without condition. Our past failures, disappointments, or rejections from others do not define us. Instead, we are defined by our identity in Christ as children of God, born anew to a life of spiritual blessing. We are accepted in Christ Jesus, and nothing can take that away.

Rejection may cause us to suffer, but that suffering is temporary—a momentary bump in the path to something greater. We have a choice in how we respond to rejection: we can let it derail us, dragging our wounds around like a ball and chain, or we can claim our heritage as children of God and move forward in grace. Scripture is full of reminders of this truth. Psalm 27:10 says, "Even if my father and mother abandon me, the LORD will always take me in." And 1 Peter 2:4 adds, "As you come to Him, the living Stone—rejected by humans but chosen and precious to God—stand confident in your faith."

To illustrate this, let's look at real-life examples of people who faced rejection and achieved greatness. Take Michael Jordan, arguably the greatest basketball player of all time. Did you know he was cut from his high school basketball team? Can you imagine that? The guy who would go on to redefine the sport was told he wasn't good enough. Throughout his career, Jordan missed more than 9,000 shots, lost nearly 300 games, and on 26 occasions, he missed the game-winning shot. But despite these setbacks, he succeeded because he didn't let rejection define him. He persevered, learned from his failures, and kept going.

Or consider Stephen King, one of the most successful writers of our time. When he submitted his first book manuscript, it was rejected 30 times. Thirty times! Frustrated, he almost gave up. He threw the manuscript in the trash, but his wife retrieved it and encouraged him to keep going. If he had let those rejections stop him, we wouldn't have the countless stories that have captivated readers for decades. But King didn't give up; now he's a household name.

Charles Spurgeon once wisely said, "God uses people who fail—because there isn't any other kind around." That quote is a powerful reminder that rejection and failure are not the end of the story. They are merely chapters in God's larger narrative in our lives.

Rejection hurts. It's painful and often leaves scars that take time to heal. But it's also a part of life, something we all experience, and God can use it for His greater purpose. Remember, rejection doesn't have the final say—God does. And in His eyes, you are loved, chosen, and accepted, no matter what the world might say. So, the next time you face rejection, whether from a job, a relationship, or even people you love, hold your head high. Trust that God has a plan; know He will never reject you. You are His, and that's a label that no one can ever take away.

Chapter 14

Never Say Never

Did you know that approximately 29 million people might say, "I will never do something," only to find themselves doing it sooner or later? It's one of those things that sneaks up on you when you least expect it. We all know the story of Judas in the Bible. He likely told himself—and maybe even Jesus—that he would never betray Him. But when the temptation of money came knocking, he did what he swore he'd never do. It's a reminder that the word "never" has a funny way of turning back on us, especially when we least expect it.

We all pledge about freedom, possessions, money, fear, reassurance, pride, and trust. We say, "I'll never do that," or "I'll always be there," but life tests those words. Take my experience, for example. Many people I once knew assured me they would stick by me no matter what, through thick and thin. They said they'd write letters, answer phone calls, and never disappoint me. But, a month later, the letters stopped coming, the calls went unanswered, and I found myself alone. It's not that they were bad people—it's just that life makes those "never" hard to keep.

I also know of a man who told his good friend he would never go on a mission trip. He wasn't interested, didn't see the point, and firmly believed it wasn't for him. But wouldn't you know it? He went, and it turned out to be one of the most transformative experiences of his life. Funny how that works, right?

Even the famous are not immune to this. J.K. Rowling once said she would never write another book about Harry Potter after the series ended. She was done, ready to move on to new things. Yet, she later published Harry Potter and the Cursed Child and continued to expand the Wizarding World universe with the Fantastic Beasts series. Then there's Richard Branson, who once said he would never enter the airline business. He was an entrepreneur, but airlines were a different ballgame. Yet, in 1984, he founded Virgin Atlantic Airways, which became a significant player in the aviation industry.

So why do we say "never"? Often, it's because we don't believe something will ever happen. We might be afraid, uncertain, or can't see it happening. Sometimes, it's because we've been told we'll never achieve anything or amount to anything. Those words can leave a deep mark; some people carry that negativity throughout their lives, believing it to be true. But others—those with grit and determination—prove the naysayers wrong.

I remember a story about a colleague from California. A teacher once told him that he would never amount to anything. He was just a kid, but those words stung. Fast forward to when he was 37 years old. He ran into that same teacher, stranded on the side of the road with a flat tire. He didn't say a word; he just helped her out, changing the tire and getting her back on her way. As he finished, he told her, "I was the child you said would never be anything. I now run a towing company, have a house and a great family." Talk about sweet revenge.

It's like how people might say they will never become a criminal, a drug addict, or an alcoholic, only to find themselves struggling with these very issues. Labels can embed "never" into almost everything people say. Being labeled a sex offender, for instance, can make someone feel like they can never be successful due to the circumstances and rules they must follow. I also remember saying my mom would never pass away or leave us, thinking I could somehow control that. I quickly learned how false that belief was. Life doesn't follow our rules or our servers.

When we say "never," we're putting limits on ourselves, and often, we're putting limits on God. We're telling Him that we know better, have things figured out, and that certain things aren't possible. But

God loves to prove us wrong. Not to boast but to show us how much He loves us and how limitless His power truly is. When we doubt Him and His ability to do something, we say His grace isn't enough, and His strength isn't made perfect in our weakness (2 Corinthians 12:9).

Look at Simon Peter, one of Jesus' closest disciples. He was a man of big words and bold promises. He once boasted that he would never be offended by Christ, never forsake Him. Yet, when the pressure was on, he did just that—denied knowing Jesus three times. After Jesus' resurrection, Peter went fishing, perhaps to clear his head or to return to something familiar. He caught nothing, but when Jesus appeared on the shore and told them to cast their nets on the other side, they were overwhelmed with fish. Peter's friend, John, recognized Jesus, and Peter, ever the impulsive one, jumped out of the boat and swam to shore. It was another impulsive act that led him back to Jesus this time. And what did Jesus do? He forgave him. Peters "never" was broken, but Jesus' love remained unshaken.

When we say, "I will never," we're making a vow—a promise that often ends up broken. Jesus demonstrated this with Peter, and life demonstrated it to us repeatedly. The Bible advises us not to make vows, not to swear by anything on earth or in heaven, but to let our "yes" be yes and our "no" be no (Matthew 5:34-37). As the Bible says, anything beyond this is from the evil one. It reminds us to be humble in our words and trust in God's plan, even when we don't understand it.

But here's the good news: when God says "never," it's a guarantee that will never be broken. 1 Kings 8:56 says, "There has not failed one word of all His good promises, which He spoke by Moses, His servant." Joshua 21:45 confirms, "Not one of all the LORD's good promises to Israel failed; everyone was fulfilled." God's promises are rock solid. We can take that to the bank when He says He'll never leave or forsake us. When He says He'll never let us down, we can trust that completely.

So the next time you catch yourself saying, "I'll never do that," or "That will never happen," take a moment to pause. Remember that life is full of surprises, and God's plans are often far beyond what we can see or imagine. Trust in His promises because his "never" is the only one that truly stands the test of time.

Chapter 15

Labeled, But Not a Failure

We need to confront a complicated and sobering truth: we will fail. This isn't a statement of defeat but an acknowledgment of our human condition. Why do we forget? Because every day, we battle against sin and the desires of the flesh. Despite our best intentions and deepest commitments, sin can still be enticing. Even the apostle Paul, a pillar of the Christian faith, captures this inner struggle vividly in Romans 7:18-19: "For I have the desire to do what is right, but not the ability to carry it out. For I do not do the good I want, but the evil I do not want is what I keep on doing." Here, Paul lays bare the reality that the battle between sin and flesh is not just theoretical; it's real, relentless, and ongoing, even for believers who strive to live in righteousness.

As Christians, we often carry the weight of our shortcomings, burdened by the knowledge that we still fall into sin and fail to live perfectly because of the sin that dwells within us. This struggle becomes even more pronounced for those who live with labels—stigmas that society or our past actions have attached to us. These labels can feel like chains, binding us to a narrative of permanent failure, with some people even hoping we'll remain in that state to confirm their doubts about us.

I know this struggle intimately. I've faced it in the most personal aspects of my life. I failed as a father, as a son, as a brother, and as a husband. I once heard someone from my past say, "Tony, I didn't know where you were going in your life." And with all the honesty I could muster, I replied, "I didn't either." If my life wasn't revolving around sports, I felt like I was falling short. And I'm confident I'm not alone in this. Many of us have faced similar feelings of failure, especially when the world is quick to slap a label on us.

But failure, while painful, is not the end of our story. Take Tim Tebow as an example. He was labeled a gimmick player and criticized for failing to succeed in the NFL. When his career in professional football didn't last long, it gave many the satisfaction of saying, "I told you so." But God had a different plan for Tebow that went far beyond the football field. Tebow has become a powerful testimony to the world through his unwavering faith and willingness to serve others. Here's how God has used him:

- *Faith: Tebow has never shied away from sharing his Christian faith. Whether in interviews, speeches, or social media, he boldly proclaims his belief in Jesus Christ.*
- *Philanthropy: Through the Tim Tebow Foundation, he has engaged in charitable work that has touched countless lives. This includes serving children with special needs and organizing "Night to Shine," an unforgettable prom night experience for people with special needs.*
- *Missions and Outreach: Tebow has participated in missionary work, building hospitals, supporting orphanages, and providing much-needed medical care to the underprivileged.*
- *Motivational Speaking: He uses his platform to inspire others, sharing messages of faith, perseverance, and the power of God's love.*
- *Writing and Books: Tebow has authored books discussing his faith journey, lessons, and how God has shaped his life.*
- *Role Model: Above all, he strives to live as a positive example of letting faith guide every aspect of one's life.*

Tebow's life is a testament to the truth in Psalm 37:23-24: "The LORD directs the steps of the godly. He delights in every detail of their lives. Though they stumble, they will never fall, for the LORD holds them by the hand." These words are not just for Tim Tebow but for all of us. To fail is human, but to be a "failure" is surrendering to defeat and refusing to rise again. As believers, we sometimes fall into the trap of thinking that our relationship with God should make us immune to failure, but that's not how God works. Often, He allows us to stumble so that we might grow, learn, and have our faith tested and strengthened.

Consider this: when a child is told not to touch a hot stove and does so anyway, the burn teaches them a valuable lesson. Similarly, God sometimes allows us to face the consequences of our actions to learn and avoid making the same mistakes again. But if we don't take those lessons to heart, we may stumble repeatedly. Yet, through the grace of Jesus Christ, when we place our faith in Him and confess our sins, we are not left in our failure. We are cleansed, forgiven, and counted as righteous in God's eyes. As Proverbs 24:16 reminds us, "Though the righteous fall seven times, they rise again, but the wicked stumble when calamity strikes."

Think of Jonah, who was initially labeled a failure for disobeying God's command to preach to Nineveh. He ran in the opposite direction, only to find himself in the belly of a great fish. But God didn't leave him there. Jonah eventually obeyed, delivered God's message, and witnessed the repentance of an entire city. Or consider Moses, who was labeled a failure after killing an Egyptian and fleeing into the wilderness. Yet God chose him to lead His people, deliver the Ten Commandments, and guide the Israelites to the Promised Land.

These stories remind us that society may try to label us—whether as drug addicts, alcoholics, cheaters, or sex offenders—but these labels do not bind God. He sees our potential, our worth, and our future through the lens of His grace. He can use our trials and failures to build character and shape us into spiritually grounded individuals who are more than the sum of our past mistakes. Our failures do not define us; God's grace and redemption do.

So, when the world tries to convince you that your failures are final, remember that your past does not limit God's plan for you. He is a God of new beginnings, second chances, and infinite mercy. Through Him, you can rise repeatedly, no matter how many times you fall. Let your story be of perseverance, faith in adversity, and the transformative power of God's love.

Chapter 16

Shoot your shot

We've all experienced those pivotal moments when we were encouraged to take a shot at something—whether it's pursuing a romantic interest, seizing a life-changing opportunity, or stepping out of our comfort zone to chase a long-held dream. The phrase "shoot your shot" is more than just a catchy saying; it's a call to boldness, a directive to take action even when doubt and fear threaten to paralyze us. It's an invitation to embrace the unknown and trust that the outcome, no matter what it may be, will be worth the risk.

Consider my son as a prime example. At just 14 years old and already towering at 6'1", he often gets asked if he plays basketball. When he used to reply, "Only in my free time," people would immediately follow up with, "Why don't you try out for the team?" Now, you might think that with his height and potential, trying out would be a no-brainer. But he hesitated. He wrestled with the same fears that plague all of us—the fear of not being good enough, failing in front of others, and not living up to expectations. Yet, despite these fears, he chose to shoot his shot. He took that leap of faith and tried out for the team. It wasn't just about basketball but about stepping into the unknown and opening himself up to new possibilities. And that's what life is often about—taking the shot, even when you're not sure where it will lead.

But let's be honest: not every shot lands where we want it to. Missing the shot is an inevitable part of life. The Bible is full of examples of missed opportunities. In Mark 10:17-22, the Rich Young Ruler missed his chance to follow Jesus because he couldn't let go of his wealth. He walked away sorrowfully, clinging to his possessions, and missed out on the eternal treasure offered to him. King Saul, another tragic figure, missed his shot as king by disobeying God's command. His disobedience led to his rejection by God and the rise of David, a man after God's heart, who would become one of Israel's most fabulous kings (1 Samuel 15). These stories remind us that missed opportunities often stem from our inability to act or our overwhelming fear of failure.

But here's the crucial point: taking the shot, despite the risks, can lead to extraordinary and life-altering outcomes. A Navy SEAL sniper, Chris Kyle offers a powerful example of this. Kyle took a shot from 2,100 yards away—the longest recorded sniper shot. Despite not seeing his target clearly, he took the shot and eliminated a significant threat to his team. This wasn't just a matter of skill but an act of faith. Kyle believed that God guided and protected him, even when the outcome was uncertain. This story resonates deeply with the truth of Hebrews 11:1, which tells us that "faith is the assurance of things hoped for, the conviction of things not seen." Sometimes, faith is about taking the shot even when you can't see where it will land, trusting that God will guide it to its intended destination.

The Bible is filled with stories of individuals who took their shots, guided by faith and the assurance that God was with them:

- *David: A young shepherd boy who faced the giant Goliath with nothing but a slingshot and a few stones. Despite the overwhelming odds, he took the shot that delivered Israel from its greatest enemy at the time. David's victory wasn't just about defeating a giant; it was about demonstrating the power of faith in God's strength over human might (1 Samuel 17:48-49).*

- *Jonathan: With boldness and unwavering trust in God, Jonathan attacked a Philistine outpost with just his armor-bearer by his side. His faith and courage led to a surprising victory, showing that God doesn't need large numbers to accomplish His will—He needs faith and action (1 Samuel 14:6).*

- *Esther: In a moment of crisis, Esther risked her life by approaching the king without being summoned, which could have led to her death. She did this to plead for the salvation of her people. Her courage and willingness to take the shot led to the deliverance of the Jewish nation from certain destruction. Esther's story is a powerful reminder that sometimes, the most significant victories require us to take the greatest risks (Esther 4:16).*

- *Peter: On the day of Pentecost, Peter stood up and boldly preached to the crowd despite the danger and opposition. His boldness and faith led to about three thousand people being added to the number of believers that day. Peter's willingness to take the shot and step into his calling with confidence changed the course of history for the early church (Acts 2:14).*

- *Paul: After being stoned and left for dead, Paul didn't give up. Instead, he got up and continued his mission to spread the Gospel, undeterred by the opposition he faced. His dedication and willingness to take shots, even in extreme adversity, transformed the early church and spread the Gospel far and wide. Paul's story is of relentless faith and courage, showing us that even when knocked down, we must get up and keep going (Acts 14:19-20).*

These stories teach us that even when carrying a label or feeling unworthy, taking the shot is a powerful testament to your faith and potential. The biggest failure is not trying at all. Chris Kyle's remarkable shot underscores the importance of seizing opportunities when they present themselves, even when the risks seem overwhelming.

"Don't let the fear of what could happen make nothing happen." This quote by Doe Zantamata is more than just a catchy phrase; it's a battle cry for anyone who has ever let fear stand in the way of their dreams. Fear is a powerful force, but it's not as powerful as the grace of God. Don't let fear paralyze you. Don't let it prevent you from seizing opportunities that could change your life. God's grace and redemption are more significant than any fear and can transform any situation.

So, shoot your shot. Whether it's in your personal life, career, relationships, or walk with God, leap. Step out confidently, knowing that even if you miss, God is there to catch you, guide your path, and open new doors. The most important thing is that you tried, had the faith to step out, and didn't let fear hold you back. In the end, those shots—the ones taken in faith, with confidence in God's plan—shape our lives and bring us closer to the extraordinary purposes He has for us.

When you take that shot, you declare that you believe in the potential of what could be, not just in the safety of what is. You're embracing the adventure of faith, where the journey is just as important as the destination. And as you move forward, remember this: God's plans for you are more significant than anything you could imagine. Each shot you take, each risk you embrace, is a step toward becoming the person God created you to be. So, confidently shoot your shot, and trust that God will do the rest.

Chapter 17

<u>Built on the Rock</u>

In Matthew 7:24-27, Jesus presents a powerful parable about two builders: wise and foolish. The wise builder constructs his house on a rock, a firm, and unyielding foundation, ensuring that when the storms of life rage, his house remains unshaken. In contrast, the foolish builder chooses to build on sand, an unstable and shifting ground, leading to the inevitable collapse of his home when adversity strikes. This parable is a profound reminder of the importance of establishing a solid foundation rooted in faith, wisdom, and unwavering trust in God.

Our feelings, doubts, and the pressures of daily life often pull us away from God's teachings. We are tempted to build our lives on the shifting sands of temporary satisfaction, material success, or fleeting pleasures. I know this all too well because I have been that foolish builder, repeatedly constructing and reconstructing my life on unstable foundations. I made decisions based on immediate gratification, thinking I could easily reset and start over if things went wrong. But life, as I discovered, doesn't work that way. The more I tried to rebuild on my terms, the more my life resembled a house teetering on the edge of collapse, vulnerable to every storm that came my way.

It was only after experiencing this cycle of failure—over and over again—that I realized my mistakes. I reflected on the story of Judas Iscariot, a man who had every opportunity to build his life on a solid foundation but ultimately chose otherwise. Judas walked with Jesus, heard His teachings, and witnessed His miracles, yet his heart was not aligned with Christ. He made choices that led to his downfall, betraying the foundation he could have built his life upon.

In many ways, I was like Judas. Outwardly, I appeared to have faith—I attended church, listened to sermons, and even spoke about God's love. But inwardly, my heart was divided. I was selective in my obedience, following the teachings of Jesus only when it was convenient for me. This selective faith led to repeated failures, a life of constant rebuilding on a shaky foundation that could never withstand the storms.

Everything changed when I encountered Billy Graham's message. His words were more than just a sermon; they were a lifeline. Billy Graham spoke with such passion and conviction that I truly listened for the first time in my life. His message pierced through the walls of self-deception I had built around my heart. Then, I decided to make my life on a firmer foundation grounded in Christ's teachings and love.

This transformation wasn't instantaneous; it was a process that required time, practice, and the unlearning of old habits. Just as overcoming destructive habits like smoking or lying takes persistent effort, building a solid foundation in faith demands dedication and patience. There were moments of doubt and times when I was tempted to revert to my old ways, but the more I invested in my relationship with Christ, the more I realized the importance of a strong foundation. I learned that actual change is gradual and often painful but also profoundly rewarding.

Years later, I began to see the fruits of building my life on a solid foundation. The difference was nothing short of miraculous. By placing my trust in Jesus Christ, I found the strength to face life's storms with a newfound resilience. The waves that once threatened to destroy me now seemed more minor, less intimidating. I had built my life on the rock of God's word, and in doing so, I discovered a stability and peace that I had never known before.

In this world, you can build your life on wealth, relationships, success, or pleasure. But only a foundation based on the word of God will stand firm against the inevitable storms. As TobyMac wisely said, "You don't need to know where you're going if you know God is leading you." This simple yet profound truth is the essence of faith. When you trust in God and build your life on His word, you can face any challenge with confidence. You may not always know the path ahead, but you can be sure that the foundation beneath your feet is unshakeable.

This is the ultimate reassurance, the unwavering promise of faith: when we build our lives on Christ, we build on a foundation that will endure. No storm, trial, or adversity can shake us when our lives are anchored in Him. Trust in God, build on His word, and you will find stability, purpose, and peace through every challenge life throws your way. This is the life that stands firm, the life built on the rock and will endure forever.

Chapter 18

Bent But Not Broken

Isaiah 42:3 says, "A bruised reed he will not break, and a faintly burning wick he will not quench." Similarly, 2 Corinthians 4:8-9 offers deep comfort: "We are afflicted in every way, but not crushed; perplexed, but not driven to despair; persecuted, but not forsaken; struck down, but not destroyed." These verses convey a profound message of hope, resilience, and restoration. They remind us that God's compassion and grace are unfailing even in our weakest and most fragile moments. He provides the strength to rebuild our lives and reignite the flame within us, no matter how dim it may seem.

The "bruised reed" and "smoldering wick" are potent symbols of spiritually, physically, or morally weak—those who feel on the verge of breaking or burning out completely. To the world, a bruised reed might seem worthless, lacking power, stability, and purpose. It's easy for society to dismiss the weak, the broken, and the wounded as expendable, to write them off as beyond repair. But God sees us differently. He sees our worth even when we are at our lowest. His love reaches out to us, offering a chance for renewal and restoration.

When I was released from prison, I felt the weight of this stigma acutely. I was viewed as a bruised reed, someone society deemed unworthy of a second chance. My label made it difficult for others to see beyond my past mistakes and recognize the possibility of redemption and change within me. It was as if my life, like a smoldering wick, was about to be extinguished. People hesitated to engage with me, allowing me to show who I was. This experience of feeling discarded and marginalized is not unique to me; it resonates with many who carry the heavy burden of societal labels.

In these moments of despair, when the world seems to turn its back on us, we must remember the words of John in 1 John 2:15, "Do not love the world or anything in the world. If anyone loves the world, love for the Father is not in them." Romans 12:2 further instructs us, "Do not conform to the pattern of this world but be transformed by the renewing of your mind." These verses remind us to look beyond the world's judgments and labels and to align ourselves with God's will. In doing so, we find our identity and purpose, not in the opinions of others but in the love and grace of our Heavenly Father.

The world often defines people by their weakest moments, by their failures, and by the mistakes they have made. But God defines us by our potential, by the love He has for us, and by the purpose He has placed within us. The bruised reed, though fragile, still has life. The smoldering wick, though faint, still holds the potential to burn brightly. And so, it is with us. No matter how broken or defeated we may feel, God's power and love can restore us, renew us, and set us on a path of purpose and fulfillment.

The Bible is filled with stories of people who, like bruised reeds and smoldering wicks, were on the brink of giving up yet found hope and restoration in God. Consider the man with the withered hand in Matthew 12. Despite the religious leaders' objections, Jesus healed him, restoring his hand, dignity, and place in society. Or the woman caught in adultery in John 8. She was dragged before Jesus, not for justice but to be condemned. Yet, instead of condemnation, she found forgiveness and a new beginning. Jesus' words, "Neither do I condemn you; go, and from now on, sin no more," were not just a dismissal of her past but an invitation to a future filled with grace and renewal.

There's also Jairus' daughter in Luke 8, who was brought back to life by Jesus. For her family, all hope was lost, but Jesus restored not just her life but also their faith. Similarly, the woman with the issue of blood, who had suffered for twelve years, found healing simply by touching Jesus' garment. Though small and fragile, her faith was enough to ignite a miracle in her life, like a smoldering wick. Even Peter, who denied Jesus three times, was renewed and given a pivotal role in the early Church after the resurrection. Each of these individuals was, in a sense, a bruised reed or a smoldering wick, yet Jesus offered them hope, healing, and restoration.

My mother, a single mother of two, exemplified this strength and resilience in the face of adversity. Despite the immense challenges she faced, she never gave up. She often attributed her ability to persevere to God's unwavering support. She would tell me, "Without God's strength, I would have broken." Her faith was a testament to the truth that even in our weakest moments, God's strength is made perfect. The same God who has the power to shape mountains and move nations is also tender enough to hold the weakest among us close to His heart, nurturing us back to strength.

This assurance is a beacon of hope for all of us. We can trust that God is powerful and tender in our pain and confusion. He can heal our deepest wounds and desires to care for us in our moments of greatest need. He doesn't see us through the lens of our sins or our failures because those have been paid for and cast away through Christ. Instead, He sees us as His redeemed children, beloved and precious, eager to run to Him and cry out, "Abba Father!"—a term of deep intimacy and trust, meaning "Daddy."

In this truth, we can find comfort and confidence. We can approach God without fear of rejection or condemnation, knowing He welcomes us with open arms. The sin, the shame, the labels that once defined us are gone, washed away by the blood of Christ. What remains is the embrace of a loving Father, who invites us to find solace, strength, and renewal in Him. No matter how bruised or smoldering we may feel, God's grace assures us that we are never beyond repair. We are His and find restoration and new life in His hands.

Understanding God's unwavering love and support gives us the courage to rebuild our lives on a firm foundation. Just as Jesus described in Matthew 7:24-27, the wise builder who constructs his house on the rock can withstand the storms of life. When we build our lives on the solid foundation of God's word and promises, we can face any trial or storm without fear of being crushed or destroyed. Even when the world labels us failures or tries to break us down, we can stand firm, knowing that our foundation is unshakable because it is built on Christ.

We must first renew our minds to build on this foundation, as Romans 12:2 instructs us. This transformation is about changing our thoughts and realigning our lives with God's will and purpose. It means letting go of the world's expectations and embracing God's truth. It means trusting that God will lift us no matter how often we fall. It means believing that, in God's eyes, we are not defined by our past mistakes or the labels others place on us but by His love and His plan for our lives.

This process of rebuilding and renewing is not easy. It takes time, effort, and a deep reliance on God. But as we commit ourselves to this journey, we will begin to see the fruits of our labor. We will see how God turns our brokenness into something beautiful. We will experience the joy of being used by God to accomplish His purposes. And we will find the strength to keep moving forward, no matter the challenges.

So, if you feel like a bruised reed or a smoldering wick today, take heart. Know that God sees you, loves you, and has a plan for you. He will not break you or snuff you out. Instead, He will nurture you, strengthen you, and restore you. He will help you build your life on a firm foundation and guide you every step of the way. Trust in Him, lean on His promises, and watch as He turns your weakness into strength, your brokenness into beauty, and your despair into hope.

Chapter 19

Unstuck

Many people feel trapped, believing that breaking free is impossible. My mom was one of those people. When she was enduring abuse from my father, she felt stuck, primarily out of fear. As a mother of two, she was caught in a cycle of helplessness and dread, feeling like there was no way out. The constant fear of his return overshadows the fleeting moments of relief when he wasn't around. Her feeling of being trapped wasn't just rooted in fear; it was also tied to a sense of failure, as though she couldn't find a way to escape the life she was in. This feeling of being stuck can manifest in many ways, often leading people to feel powerless against their circumstances or even their behaviors.

Similarly, some people find themselves trapped in sinful ways, unable to break free from habits that harm them and those around them. For me, it was the sin of lust that kept me confined. I felt trapped by my desire for relationships with multiple women, something I had grown up seeing and came to accept as usual. Even though I knew it was wrong, the loneliness and powerlessness I felt kept me in that cycle. I was stuck, feeling guilty and ashamed every day, yet unable to envision a way out. The thought of change was terrifying, mainly because it required confronting parts of myself that I had always avoided. The discomfort of facing my sins and the effort needed to change created a resistance within me, keeping me stuck in that destructive cycle.

This phenomenon, known as perseveration, is where someone continues a thought or behavior even after the original stimulus is gone. It's like being caught in a loop, repeating the same actions and expecting different results, yet feeling unable to break free. For *example, I once met someone in jail who was caught in a cycle of stealing. He would be released, only to return shortly after, often for the same crime. When I asked him why he couldn't break free from this pattern, he confessed that it was easier to steal drug money than to work for it. He feared change and the unknown, which trapped him in his lifestyle. Tragically, he was recently caught stealing a bicycle from a child. His story is a stark reminder of how powerful the chains of sin and bad habits can be and how difficult it can be to break free.*

Being labeled can often make a person feel trapped, especially when those labels are imposed by others or oneself. Labels can act as barriers, restricting identity, opportunities, and self-perception. This sense of restriction often stems from a perceived lack of trust or belief from others, which can diminish one's confidence and potential. I speak from experience because I know what it's like to live with a label and the barriers it creates, making it feel impossible to move forward or change. But we don't have to remain trapped.

The Bible contains numerous stories of people who were "stuck" in difficult situations but were ultimately freed through faith, divine intervention, or wise action. These stories are powerful reminders that God can liberate us from any situation, no matter how hopeless it may seem.

1. *Moses and the Israelites at the Red Sea:*
   - *Situation: The Israelites were trapped between the Red Sea and the pursuing Egyptian army.*
   - *Resolution: God parted the Red Sea, allowing the Israelites to escape while the sea closed over the Egyptians (Exodus 14). This miraculous event shows that God can make a way when we feel there's no way out.*
2. *Joseph in Egypt:*
   - *Situation: Joseph was sold into slavery by his*

brothers and later imprisoned on false charges.
- *Resolution: Joseph became Egypt's second-most powerful man through God's providence, eventually saving his family and many others from famine (Genesis 37–50). His story reminds us that God can turn our situation around for good even when betrayed and mistreated.*

3. *Daniel in the Lion's Den:*
- *Situation: Daniel was thrown into a den of lions for praying to God, defying the king's decree.*
- *Resolution: God shut the mouths of the lions, and Daniel was unharmed. The next day, he was released, and his accusers were punished (Daniel 6). Daniel's unwavering faith in God delivered him from what seemed like a certain death.*

4. *Paul and Silas in Prison:*
- *Situation: Paul and Silas were imprisoned for preaching the gospel.*
- *Resolution: An earthquake miraculously opened the prison doors, and the jailer, moved by their faith, converted to Christianity (Acts 16:25-34). This story illustrates that God's power can free us even in the darkest, most confining places.*

5. *The Israelites in the Wilderness:*
- *Situation: After leaving Egypt, the Israelites were stuck in the wilderness, struggling with hunger, thirst, and doubt.*
- *Resolution: God provided manna, water from a rock, and guidance through Moses to lead them to the Promised Land (Exodus 16-17, Numbers 20). This journey, though difficult, was marked by God's constant provision and direction, reminding*

us that He is with us every step of the way.

These stories remind us that we don't have to remain stuck in sinful ways or difficult situations. We can find clarity, freedom, and renewed purpose by trusting God and seeking His guidance. Just as the Israelites were led through the Red Sea, God can part the waters in our lives, making a way where there seems to be none. Just as Joseph was lifted from the pit to a place of prominence, God can elevate us from our lowest points to heights we never imagined. And just as Paul and Silas were freed from their chains, God can break the chains that bind us, whether physical, emotional, or spiritual.

Although I was once trapped in my habitual sin, I found liberation in 2015 by trusting God. It wasn't an instant transformation; it took patience, faith in His timing, and a willingness to confront the parts of myself I had long ignored. But ultimately, I was freed from my cycle of sin. This freedom is not just available to me; it's available to anyone who feels stuck in drugs, porn, alcohol, lust, or any other habitual sin. The key is relying on God's grace, seeking His guidance, and intentionally trying to change. These steps can help break the chains of recurring patterns of sin and lead to a transformed and fulfilling life.

Remember, God's grace is sufficient for overcoming habitual sin. His forgiveness isn't just for our initial repentance but for our ongoing struggles. As 2 Corinthians 12:9 states, "My grace is sufficient for you, for my power is made perfect in weakness." God's power shines the brightest in our moments of greatest weakness. Therefore, like Paul, we can gladly boast about our weaknesses so Christ's power may rest on us.

We are not defined by our sins or the labels others place on us. We are defined by God's grace and the transformative power of His love. No matter how trapped we may feel, God offers a way out. No matter how broken we may be, God provides healing and restoration. We can trust that, through Him, we can break free from anything that holds us back and step into the fullness of the life He has planned for us.

Chapter 20

<u>*Faith, Fight, Finish*</u>

As we conclude this chapter, I want to focus on three guiding principles we should all strive to embody daily: Faith, Fight, and Finish. These aren't just words; they are potent forces that can guide us through life's most daunting challenges, pushing us to overcome obstacles, rise above adversity, and live purposefully.

Let me share the story of someone I deeply admire who embodies these principles. Despite not being labeled a criminal, he faced intense scrutiny and was often judged harshly by those who didn't believe in him. They called him awful, terrible, and a lousy thrower. He struggled to get noticed by college recruiters but never doubted his ability or worth. His perseverance eventually paid off when Mississippi State took a chance on him. But even after this small victory, his life was far from easy.

In 2013, he lost his mother to stage four cancer. She was his best friend, mother, supporter, and biggest cheerleader. Her loss was a devastating blow, a reminder of the fragility of life and the pain of losing someone so irreplaceable. Yet, even in her final moments, she left him with words that would shape his future: "Let me be your story." These words were a powerful reminder that the labels others imposed on him did not define his identity. Instead, his identity was shaped by the love, strength, and legacy his mother had passed on to him—a story that was his to tell.

In her honor and in memory of his brother, who tragically took his own life, he founded the "Faith, Fight, Finish" foundation. Through this foundation, he continues to carry forward the legacy of his mother and brother, using their stories to inspire others to keep pushing forward, no matter the odds. I resonate with his journey deeply because, in many ways, it mirrors my own. While our circumstances differ—his challenges in football and dealing with the loss of loved ones versus my struggles with loss and the battles I've faced—the impact on our lives is strikingly similar.

My mother, much like his, was a woman of incredible faith. As a single mother of two, she demonstrated strength, hard work, love, care, and an unwavering fear of God. She was a fighter, battling daily to provide for us, guide us, and ensure we had a hopeful future. Even in her most challenging moments, she never lost faith. With all her heart, she believed that God would move mountains in His time. Her fight was fierce and relentless, even when cancer came into our lives. We feared it might be a battle she couldn't win, but she faced it head-on with the same unyielding courage she showed in everything she did. Though she ultimately passed away suddenly from a heart attack, a battle she couldn't anticipate or fight, her legacy of faith, strength, and love continues to shape who I am today.

In 1 Timothy 6:12, Paul urges us to "Fight the good fight of the faith. Take hold of the eternal life to which you were called and about which you made the good confession in the presence of many witnesses." This is precisely what my mother did. She fought the good fight with unwavering faith, holding on to the promise of eternal life. Just as Paul reflects in 2 Timothy 4:7, "I have fought the good fight, I have finished the race, I have kept the faith," so did she. Her journey was marked by faith, courage, and a steadfast commitment to the path laid before her. She fought with all her heart, finished her race with honor, and kept the faith until the very end.

Now, let's break down what it means to live by Faith, Fight, and Finish:

Faith is more than a belief; it's the foundation of everything we do. Hebrews 11:1 says, "Now faith is the assurance of things hoped for, the conviction of things not seen." Faith means trusting God, even when the road ahead is unclear. It means believing in His promises, even when we can't see the outcome. For some, faith is trusting that a loved one will recover or that a difficult situation will improve. For others, it's the quiet confidence that God is leading them, even when the world is uncertain. Faith allows us to keep going when everything else tells us to stop. It's the anchor that holds us steady through life's storms.

Fight is the willingness to stand up against the forces that seek to pull us down. Life is a battle, and we face daily challenges that test our resolve. But what matters is not the size of the challenge but the strength of our determination. All Christians are called to fight spiritually. God provides us the necessary armor (Ephesians 6:10–17) to battle sin, resist temptation, and stand firm in our faith. The spiritual fight is not easy, but it's necessary. It's about confronting our demons, whether they be addictions, fears, or doubts, and refusing to let them dictate our lives. Every day, I fought against the urge to fall back into old habits that once threatened to tear my family apart. I knew that giving in would only deepen the wounds I had already caused. It was a battle I had to fight within myself. But I had to want to fight if I wanted to change. And that's what it takes: the will to fight for what is right, what we believe in, and what we love.

The finish is the culmination of our journey. It's about crossing the finish line and how we finish. Do we give up when things get tough, or do we press on, determined to complete what we've started? Life is filled with moments where we want to throw in the towel, but finishing strong is about resilience and perseverance. It's about honoring those who have believed in us by refusing to give up. My mother's support, love, and belief in me didn't end with her passing—they fueled me forward. I finish this journey for her, honoring the love she poured into me and demonstrating that even in overwhelming loss, we can find the strength to carry on and complete our stories with grace and courage. Finishing isn't just about reaching the end—it's about doing so with the same spirit and determination that carried us through the most challenging times.

And my journey isn't finished yet. God has reunited me with my kids, and my youngest son has been baptized. So, I encourage you to keep the faith, keep fighting, and finish the journey God has set before you. Remember, the race isn't given to the swift but to those who endure.

About the Author

As an author, I hope my writing will resonate beyond the page, reaching hearts meaningfully. I'm not just telling stories; I'm sharing pieces of myself—my lessons, struggles, and triumphs—with the hope that someone out there will find comfort, strength, and inspiration.

I pray that these pages remind you that you are not alone in your journey and that there is always hope even in moments of uncertainty. Not only that, but I've learned that life isn't about perfection but about perseverance and the beauty of getting back up after a fall. If my words can inspire even one person to keep going, to chase their dreams, or to believe in their resilience, then every late night and every ounce of effort has been worth it.

To anyone reading this, know that your story matters. You can inspire others through words, actions, or quiet acts of courage. Never underestimate the impact you can have. I pray that my books serve as a reminder of that truth, a spark of encouragement that helps light your path forward.

Read more at https://antonio-banks.ck.page/d3e3da6d72?fbclid=IwY2xjawFj3NdleHRuA2FlbQIxMQABHWuK8F5Syf

9 798822 793560